Jossey-Bass Teacher

Jossey-Bass Teacher provides educators with practical knowledge and tools to create a positive and lifelong impact on student learning. We offer classroom-tested and research-based teaching resources for a variety of grade levels and subject areas. Whether you are an aspiring, new, or veteran teacher, we want to help you make every teaching day your best.

From ready-to-use classroom activities to the latest teaching framework, our value-packed books provide insightful, practical, and comprehensive materials on the topics that matter most to K–12 teachers. We hope to become your trusted source for the best ideas from the most experienced and respected experts in the field.

Dedication

I dedicate this book to the dreamers; all those lovers of fantasy and fable who still believe they can make a difference—and do.

JB JOSSEY-BASS

Adventures in Fantasy

Lessons and Activities in Narrative and Descriptive Writing, Grades 5–9

John Gust

BICENTENNIAL
1807
WILEY
2007
BICENTENNIAL

John Wiley & Sons, Inc.

Published by Jossey-Bass
A Wiley Imprint
989 Market Street, San Francisco, CA 94103-1741 www.josseybass.com

Wiley Bicentennial logo: Richard J. Pacifico

Jossey-Bass books and products are available through most bookstores. To contact Jossey-Bass directly call our Customer Care Department within the U.S. at 800-956-7739, outside the U.S. at 317-572-3986, or fax 317-572-4002.

Jossey-Bass also publishes its books in a variety of electronic formats. Some content that appears in print may not be available in electronic books.

ISBN: 978-0-7879-9290-3

Printed in the United States of America
FIRST EDITION
PB PRINTING   10 9 8 7 6 5 4 3 2 1

About This Book

Adventures in Fantasy is a progressive series of ready-to-use lessons and activities that will guide your students through the steps necessary to first create and then write their own original work of fantasy. Your student writers will embark on a hero's journey; their very own write of passage.

With chapters such as "Threading the Theme," "Forming the Fantasyland," "Setting the Surroundings," "Crafting the Characters," "Plotting the Path," "Wording the Wonders," "Sketching the Scenes," and "Trimming the Tale," students will learn the process involved in creating their own fantasy adventure, while also acquiring many excellent story writing skills along the way.

In this resource students will first learn to draw their very own fantasyland map. The lessons on map-making skills are sure to make the task easier. Then students will learn how to use plenty of sensory details, mood, and transition words to write a highly descriptive Travelogue that will guide the reader on a journey to a number of mysterious settings on their land. Once the surroundings are set, students will begin crafting a clever cast of characters. To get your students started, there are even examples of different types of fantasy characters and creatures. After the characters are cast, students will next develop a plot line of the journey their story's hero will take. With the path of the protagonist clearly laid, students will then commence writing their story. They will have appeased the powers that guide the threshold to the underworld and now be allowed to dive into the wonderful world of narrative.

There are lessons on figurative writing, showing not telling, dialogue, alliteration, onomatopoeia, and more. Plus there are plenty of rubrics to make the storytelling experience and revision process all that much easier.

When the story is complete, your student writers will now be just like the heroes they have created in their very own fantasy story! And what will be the boon that they will receive for all their heroic efforts? The published book, of course. Try the bookmaking lesson and give your students the boon, the reward, they deserve.

About the Author

John Gust is a fifth-grade teacher in the Los Angeles Unified School District and an adjunct faculty member at Antioch University, Los Angeles. He has published numerous books on topics ranging from self-esteem enhancement, to character development, to systems thinking, to communication skills and multicultural education. John's first attempt at storytelling was a personal narrative titled *Round Peg, Square Hole: A Teacher Lives and Learns in Watts* (Heinemann, 1999). Currently, John is busy at work writing a fantasy trilogy for young adults. For more information about John Gust, his writing workshops, and his other books, please visit www.johngust.org.

Acknowledgments

I would like to thank the PTA at Lomita Magnet Elementary School for buying my fifth-grade classroom that first set of *The Hobbit*. That wonderful book got the whole project started. And since we're talking about *The Hobbit*, I might as well thank J.R.R. Tolkien himself. Sure do love his stories. In fact, I'd like to thank all of the fantasy writers out there who have added so much imaginative fun to my days of reading and writing in the classroom. That includes my own fantasy writing and reading students, as well! Reading your stories, and the stories of the great authors we have read together, has been the most fun of all. So thanks. You guys are flat out awesome!

I would like to thank Barbara Branscomb, the principal at Lomita Magnet Elementary. In spite of some heavy pressure to implement a mandated language arts program, Barbara gave me the freedom to dive into this wonderful world of fantasy. I think she knew all along that I would need to fantasize at least *some* of my day away if I was going to survive the jungle of the Los Angeles Unified School District. And while I'm at it, I would like to acknowledge the LAUSD, and my students' parents, for giving me the classroom and the young companions with which to experience these many exciting adventures in fantasy.

Finally, I would like to thank Jossey-Bass—the editorial team, Christie Hakim, Julia Parmer, Pamela Berkman, designer Chris Wallace, and illustrators Gary Mohrman and Neal Armstrong—for guiding the book to its final form and providing the opportunity to distribute these ideas and resources.

Contents

Chapter 6: Plotting the Path 121

Chapter 7: Wording the Wonders 151

Chapter 8: Sketching the Scene   185

Chapter 9: Starting the Story   203

Chapter 10: Trimming the Tale   227

Chapter 11: Booking the Boon   235

Introduction

Fairy tales are more than true: not because they tell us that dragons exist, but because they tell us that dragons can be beaten.

—G. K. Chesterson

In the Los Angeles Unified School District where the language arts curriculum has been overtaken by one-size-fits-all basal reading programs, official curriculum checkers pay regular visits to classrooms to make certain that scripted lessons are transmitted according to schedule, student essays are written on demand, desks are arranged in the approved design, bulletin boards are displaying the appropriate content standards, and standardized test after standardized test is being properly administered. Hiding somewhere within this vast conglomerate of a system, however, is a classroom of children concealing the fact that they are reading good books. In this secreted room, after the official curriculum checkers have paid a visit to do their check, check, checking, each student reaches into his or her desk, and like a flick of a magic wand, whips out a book and dives through a portal of fluttering pages into a wonderful world of fantasy.

This is how the story and this book began: my students and I escaped. I, the teacher of a small band of thirty or so learners, got a chance to beat a dragon off of my back. As for my fifth-grade students, they embarked on a hero's quest, a read and write of passage, a uniquely subversive act. Fully aware that if we chose to read the books that we were concealing in our desks we would be going underground, doing something the district authorities frowned upon, my students were engaged as never before. Like the heroes in the stories

1

we read, in order to be the heroes they were, my students would be required to function in both worlds: the standardized, scripted, one-size-fits-all, test-prep world, and the underworld where we would follow our bliss and allow our imaginations to run free. My students, who agreed to embark on this journey, knew that they would have to both score well on the many tests that were soon to come for the standardized instruction that I was mandated to implement and complete an enormous amount of additional work—writing, thinking—just so they could read the novels of which they were so fond. My students were all for it, and more than ready to get started. So off we went on our heroes' quest, our writers' journey ... fighting this pervasive condition called "sameness," as Lois Lowry named it in *The Giver*, ... struggling against the hegemony of the one-mind called "IT" on the planet Camazotz, as created by Madeleine L'Engle in *A Wrinkle in Time*.

Now I know that not all the teachers who will choose to use this book are subjected to the same dull drone of having to implement, day in and day out, a district-mandated, standardized, scripted, one-size-fits-all basal language arts program such as the one I faced before beginning this adventure in fantasy. I know that in some school districts teachers are treated like real professionals who are held accountable for teaching the content standards that their state's department of education has, through a lengthy, democratic process, assigned to their particular grade level. I know that, in these school districts, teachers have the freedom to choose their own books and materials with which to teach the language arts content standards for which they are held accountable. I know that in some school districts teachers are allowed to use various novels, magazine and newspaper articles, opinion editorials, expository texts, and other original sources of their own choosing. I also know that not every school district has curriculum checkers who roam the hallways making sure that every teacher at grade level is on the very same lesson at the very same time, or that their classroom desks have been arranged in the pattern approved by the district, or that the bulletin boards are all posted according to regulation, or that the exact number of minutes as specified by their district are being spent per day on teaching language arts, or math, or science, or whatever. I know all these things. To those of you who are fortunate enough to have all these freedoms, I say: "Great!" "Fabulous!" "Good for you!" "Keep up the good work!" ... and "Have fun using this book!"

But for all of you who have had all these professional freedoms taken away, I'm here to say, "There's still hope!" If, like me, you're willing to take a chance to buck the system, to beat a dragon off *your* back and do something that I believe is above and beyond the ordinary, others will take notice, and those freedoms will be returned. It happened to me in that exact way. When I first began this adventure, my students and I actually had to sneak in our reading and writing of fantasy. Then, once my students' reading and writing began to significantly improve, their parents got onboard. In spite of the fact that I was supposed to be implementing a mandated language arts program, the PTA went so far as to buy my classroom a complete set of *The Hobbit*, by J.R.R. Tolkien. Emboldened by this parental support, I then actually started posting my students' fantasy writing on the classroom bulletin boards. The proper content standards addressed by the writing assignment, and the rubric that assessed their efforts, were prominently displayed adjacent to the work, of course. But nonetheless, the nonmandated work was still posted. Then, I even put aside my fears about what might happen should I get caught by the administration for not being on the specific lesson required for that particular day. No longer did we whip out our fantasy books or writing only after the official curriculum checkers left the room. I put every nonmandated activity that we were doing out in clear view for everyone and anyone to see. And do you know what? Because of the excellent work my students produced, and because of the wonderful support I received from my students' parents and my principal—who, after seeing the results, began to trust my professional judgment—I was left alone. Powerful district administrators even came into the room and looked in awe and wonder at the exemplary, nonmandated student work posted, and did nothing. Never had they seen so much terrific writing. Finally, my efforts were paying off. As for my students, and their parents who time and again told me how much their child enjoyed writing now that they had something worthy to write, actually began to think of *me* as a hero of sorts. So I say to you, fellow teachers, become a hero or heroine and take back your classroom! Put the decision-making power as to what materials and methods will be used to address your state's content standards back into the hands of the professionals who deserve it: the teachers. And enjoy this adventure in fantasy with *your* small band of student writer heroes.

Here, my students' fantasyland maps and completed stories have taken over an entire wall in the classroom.

This commentary appeared in the *Los Angeles Times* on November 6, 2004. I think of it as a dystopian, fantasy/sci-fi version of the not-too-distant future that the No Child Left Behind Act is almost certain to create.

Are Schools Building Minds or Machines?

By JOHN GUST

I am employee No. 610282. I am a teacher in the Los Angeles Unified School District. I am working at full capacity to make certain that in my classroom no child will be left behind. To accomplish this goal, I am focused on transmitting all of the state's content standards in language arts, mathematics, science, social studies, physical education, art, music and health.

Each lesson taught in my classroom is accompanied with the proper posting of the standards. Scripted lessons are read verbatim. For every item of student work posted on classroom bulletin boards, a rubric with the specific standards is provided. The mandated time per day that students spend having standards transmitted for each subject area is duly noted.

District-sanctioned bulletin boards are prominently displayed. Student desks are arranged in the pattern recommended by the district.

Student report cards are now done online. Teachers simply scroll down a long list of standardized teacher comments and choose several for the small comment box.

Throughout the course of on school year I implement six district-mandated standardized tests for language arts, four for mathematics and three for science. There is also more than a week's worth of state-mandated standardized tests.

And I do these things, for which I am held accountable, in an effort to accomplish the lofty mission of leaving no child behind. To reach this goal, all my students must reach the state proficiency level in each subject tested. Unfortunately, these measures and mechanizations will not enable us to reach that goal. So, to make certain that we do not leave any child behind, I propose the following: First, replace all textbooks with handheld computers. Teachers can download standardized course textbooks, assignments and assessments. Students can complete all work on their handhelds and simply send it back to the teachers.

Eventually, all standardized student-teacher interaction will be electronic. And all that sloppy, nonstandard face-to-face communication can be eliminated. However, even with this huge change in the way we educate our children, some will still be left behind. Therefore, something more drastic is needed.

Eventually, we will need to implement a brain augmentation process utilizing a variety of neural implants. We inject each lagging student with a solution containing nanobots. These sub-microscopic robots will then travel through the bloodstream into the brain, where they will construct a neural implant. We can then transmit all required standards directly into each child's brain.

Yet, even with this advanced technology, a few children may still be left behind. If the neural implants do not get the job done, we will need to scan each child's brain, disassemble it atom by atom and reconstruct it, giving it greater capacity, speed and reliability.

If we stay on course, we will surely reach our goal. Students will cross the human-machine divide, and then, and only then, will we leave no child behind.

John Gust is a fifth-grade teacher at a math/science magnet school.

Here, my students' plot lines of *James and the Giant Peach* have been prominently posted with accompanying standards and rubric.

Chapter One

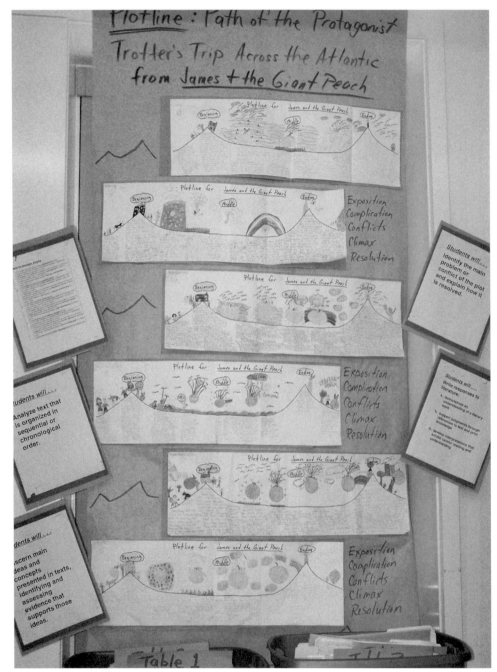

A Hero's Quest, a Writer's Journey

Fantasy is the natural, the appropriate language for the recounting of the spiritual journey and the struggle of good and evil in the soul.

—Ursula K. Le Guin

If you haven't noticed, in the last several years the popularity of fantasy and young adult fantasy has been growing by leaps and bounds: J. K. Rowling's *Harry Potter* series seems to have started the party jumping; thanks to recent movies, Tolkien's *Lord of the Rings* trilogy and C. S. Lewis's *Chronicles of Narnia* have come back to life again; Roald Dahl's *Charlie and the Chocolate Factory* and *James and the Giant Peach* have also had a resurgence of sorts; Philip Pullman's *His Dark Materials* trilogy is doing exceedingly well; Christopher Paolini's *Inheritance* series has made it big on the best-seller lists; *Dragon Rider, Inkspell,* and *Inkheart* by Cornelia Funke have all been best-sellers; the ongoing *Artemis Fowl* series by Eoin Colfer is quite popular; and Jeanne duPrau has a sturdy success with *The City of Ember* and sequel *The People of Sparks.* Fantasy is definitely in, and kids are loving it!

What I find about fantasy is that it makes it easier for teachers to take their students on a grand and adventurous journey. When reading and writing fantasy, students have a terrific opportunity to explore the imaginative worlds created by the writers whose stories they read, and to face the challenge of producing the descriptive details needed to create their own unique fantasy world in the stories they write. And in these new worlds, there's a world of learning going on.

Kids will write for long periods of time, with great effort, and with fabulous results, if you give them something they deem worthy of writing. Every year I ask my students which is their favorite form or purpose of writing. I ask: Is it to inform, educate, persuade, or entertain? They *always* pick entertainment. Fortunately, fantasy sure does entertain—abundantly.

For me, it's entertaining to sit at a table with a student, examining his newly created map, getting to know his characters, exploring his hero's journey, jumping into his story. I'm always amazed by the depth of my students' imaginations. Sometimes, however, there is a huge gap between the imagined visions that arise from their stories and what has thus far been put down on the page. I practically have to wrestle with them to get them to fill in the gaps. They've missed all kinds of descriptive detail, and action, and character thoughts and feelings, and tension that needs to be seen on paper. But that's what the writing process is for: to flush out those details, to write, and rewrite and revise, and improve. In the words of Anne Lamott, author of *Bird by Bird: Some Instructions on Writing and Life:* "It is work and play together. When they are working on their books or stories, their heads will spin with ideas and invention. They'll see the world through new eyes."

Have no doubt about it. These stories of fantasy are about a hero's quest. The quest begins with the heroes inside the stories, but it ends inside the heroes and heroines who write the stories. And the boon, the prize, that they will receive for their heroic efforts? Why, the published story, of course—a tale that just may stay with them for generations. A story to be read in later years, after they've grown up, married maybe, perhaps had a child, or grandchild, of their own.

I must admit that I harbor my own fantasies that—if I make the writing fun, important, and challenging enough—my students will take their narratives and hold onto them through the years. Perhaps, like what happened with an autobiography that I wrote while in the sixth grade, they'll lose track of their stories, but their mothers will snatch them up and keep them tucked away in some drawer, or stuffed in some lonely box up in the attic, only to be rediscovered years later like treasures in a chest. I have fantasies that—as I did when my mother brought out my old autobiography—my students, when they're all grown up, will hold their stories in their hands, remembering that it was they who wrote them, many years ago. They'll think back to how much work it took to complete the stories, how many activities and minilessons they had to endure, how many conferences it took with Mr. Gust to discuss their writing. They'll sit down, read their stories over, and then also remember how they promised Mr. Gust to read them to their children, if they ever had any, with the hope of having some of the same fun we did putting the stories together in class. Because, as I tell my students when in my class, if you read your story to your children and they're laughing—either with you or at you—at that moment you will be the hero you always knew you could be.

So I dream about them, laughing and giggling with their own children, or nieces, or nephews, grandchildren, or even, students (if they become teachers, that is). They'll be lounging in a big chair, in some cozy corner, sipping a cup of tea. And they'll have a quiet, private, heroic grin on their shining, smiling faces.

How to Use This Book

There are basically two ways to use this book. The first is to use some of the strategies and activities offered here in piecemeal fashion to provide supplemental support to your students as they complete some other narrative writing assignment. There are lessons here that can help student writers develop a narrative's theme, or describe a setting or characters, or create a plot line or use figurative language or dialogue, and more.

The second way to use this book is to treat it as a tool or vehicle that will take your student writers on a hero's quest, or a writer's journey. In this case, think of it as a template for a rite of passage—or "write" of passage, if you like. In one way, yes, the book is designed to assist student writers in passing from one way of thinking to another. Most of the students who come to me in the fifth grade don't think of themselves as writers. But I can assure you, when they have progressed through the various strategies and activities provided in this book, they most certainly do. And in spite of the many challenges they will encounter, they will enjoy the process, as well. Here is how it works:

- *What do you think of yourself as a writer?* First, before beginning, all student authors should reflect on what they think of themselves as writers. They should be given an opportunity to acknowledge past thoughts, feelings, habits, and patterns about their writing. They should think about which have limited their growth and which have supported their growth. Students need to be given time to acknowledge past feelings about their experiences as writers. Many students have a poor image of themselves as writers, and an even worse view of writing to begin with. Invite students to write the answers to these questions in a journal that they can keep throughout the journey.

- *Shed the old image.* With this clear image of themselves as writers, it is now time for students to let the image go. Students must realize that that's the writer they used to be. Find a way to help your students bury the old, negative image. Have them burn it, shred it, flush it, renounce it. Invite them to do it out loud, to do it in writing. Help them . . . let it go.

- *Begin the journey.* Now the period of trials and tribulations is upon the young writers. This will be a dramatic period of strong exertion. They will have many writing tasks to endure as they work to complete their fantasy stories. As a result, their perceptions of themselves will be forever altered.

- *Discover your new self.* With the writing started and perhaps nearing completion, begin asking your students what new thoughts they have about their writing. What new thoughts do they have about themselves as writers? Is there anything about the experience worth sharing, talking about? Let your students know how you felt watching them and their writing progress along the way. Ask your students to see themselves as the new writers that they are, standing on a mountain's peak with a distant view of their old selves as reluctant writers standing down below. What was the old self like? What does it feel like to be the new self?

- *Celebrate.* When the fantasy story and book is done . . . it's time to party! Whether it's simply with the heroic student writers in your classroom, or with added family and friends, you and your students should share your feelings of accomplishment with plenty of ceremony. Let the festivities begin!

- *Acknowledge and dedicate.* The central focus of the celebration is the author's story, the book, the boon, the gift that is offered to the family. Here is where the students give thanks to all those who have participated in the journey, and perhaps to all of those who have been influential in their lives along the way. Their acknowledgments and dedications page can even be read out loud with the offering. Ideally, most of the people mentioned will be present for the reading.

An Adventure in Fantasy

I like to think of this book and the strategies and activities included within as a type of adventure on which teachers will lead their students. As you can see from the following illustration, which shows how the remaining chapters of this book have been arranged, the journey—starting at the bottom with threading

| Booking the Boon |
| Trimming the Tale |
| Starting the Story |
| Sketching the Scenes |
| Wording the Wonders |
| Plotting the Path |
| Crafting the Characters |
| Setting the Surroundings |
| Forming the Fantasyland |
| Threading the Theme |

the story's theme, all the way to the top where students will acquire the reward for their efforts, the completed book, or boon—is much like climbing a tall, treacherous mountain. That's exactly the feeling that I want students to have when working their stories: an intense sense of accomplishment and efficacy. It should feel as if they have just scaled a great, mighty mountain.

Genres of Fantasy

The nicest small children, without the slightest
doubt, are those who have been fed upon fantasy,
and the nastiest are the ones who know all the facts.

—Roald Dahl

I'm not so sure I'd go so far as Roald Dahl in saying that the nasty kids are the ones who know all the facts, but I do know that a lot of nice children really do seem to feed on fantasy. They love it: all the many forms and subgenres of fantasy. Let's take a quick look at the many subgenres. Perhaps you'll want to teach your students about them, as well.

Epic, High, or Heroic Fantasy

This most popular form of fantasy involves a scenario in which the fate of an entire world is in the hands of the hero. It's the classic struggle of good against evil. There is also a sense of a grand destiny, where the main character—who is often either the legitimate heir to the throne or an ordinary, simple person—somehow saves or restores his or her kingdom. The hero, after gathering up a trustworthy friend and mentor, or a small band of companions, sets off on an epic quest through a land filled with awe and wonder. They're in pursuit of some object of power, such as a ring, or sword, or amulet, because gaining hold of these things will help tip the scales of power back in the right direction. Along the way, the lurking, evil force—sometimes personified in the form of a dark lord—gains power and launches a relentless campaign against them. All kinds of evil creatures crawl out of nowhere.

Often, the hero is portrayed as a magician, or a wizard in training. As the story unfolds the hero or heroine has to make a choice between using his or her powers for evil or good. In all epic, high, or heroic fantasy, the hero is tempted with all kinds of promises from the evil side. Yet, these heroes always fight to find the inner strength to make the right decision, for they know that their choices will also require some personal, lasting self-sacrifice. In the end, with much effort, unexpected help, and internal struggling, somehow these individuals prevail; they fulfill a higher purpose, and a prophecy, to become the heroes they were destined to be, saving their world, once and for all.

Adventure Fantasy

In this type of fantasy the heroes or heroines are on an adventure for the simple purpose of satisfying their own fanciful whims and desires. These heroes—who may include small adventurers like mice and moles, badgers, bunnies, or bears—crave an adventure, and by golly, you can be sure they're going to have a grand time along the way. This type of fantasy is packed full of magic and beasts, and quests for all sorts of enchanted treasures. However, in this type of fantasy, the hero's need to save an entire kingdom or world, and an epic struggle of good against evil, are missing. Instead, the tale is free to follow the freewheeling escapades of the heroes as their wishes and dreams are fulfilled. And once they get what they were after, they return home, of course. But rather than their quest ending with a defining moment that saves the world, the reader is left with the impression that the hero will venture out again, sometime soon, on yet another thrilling adventure.

Dark Fantasy

Dark fantasy includes ghost stories, horror, and gothic fiction. Ghost stories involve all kinds of weird living dead: Funny ghosts may show up and talk to people, haunting them; headless horsemen may go galloping around the countryside, taunting townsfolk; dead bodies may stumble around in search of human flesh. In most horror story plots, the evil force, or forces—ghosts, demons, or phantoms, for example—build up to an intensely scary level, thus raising the tale's tension, until the very end, when good finally prevails. In pure horror stories, anything goes, so watch out for the gore. And, finally, gothic is a particular form of fantasy that involves stories usually set in a crumbling gothic mansion, surrounded by a desolate moor. These stories usually involve an ordinary person who has been pulled into a gloomy world, forced to defend his or her honor against the ghostly inhabitants of the place.

Fairy Tales

Fairy tales are really tales of transformation. They are stories in which the protagonist goes through a massive personal change. A frog might turn into a prince, an ugly duck into a beautiful swan, a puppet into a real live boy, a maid into a princess, a stuffed bunny into a romping rabbit. The familiar theme of the fairy tale is that something beautiful and good can come from something so unsightly.

Magical Realism

In these kinds of stories magical things happen, usually without warning, in the middle of someone's very normal, everyday life. Mysterious events transpire, weird apparitions pop up out of nowhere. And when these strange things begin to happen, the protagonist's life is changed forever. After the adventure through these strange series of events, the life of the protagonist usually goes on as normal, but something inside that individual has changed. Sometimes this interior, psychological change will alter her life in a more meaningful way than anything external, or physical, ever could. She thinks of herself or the world differently, and that makes all the difference.

Magic

The magic of Faerie is not an end in itself, its virtue is in its options: among these are the satisfaction of certain primordial human desires. One of these desires is to survey the depths of space and time. Another is (as will be seen) to hold communion with other living things.

—J.R.R. Tolkien

Inevitably, your student writers are going to use magic in their stories. Fantasy and magic go hand in hand. However, magic can easily be overused. The worst thing that can happen is that the writer starts using magic at any time for just about any reason. Magic needs limits. When using magic, the writer must be very clear about the rules. Readers shouldn't be thinking that anything might happen at any time. Characters shouldn't be able to solve every problem with a simple wave of a wand. If so, what's the point of reading the story? Any time the hero gets in trouble, the reader will know that some magical trick will be thrown in to solve the problem. Ridiculous!

Magical ability and the use of magic should come at a high price. One such price could be the long and arduous training that any mage, magician, or wizard must go through. Another such price is for the character to know that she will no longer live a normal, perhaps happy, life, after its use. Sometimes, the price is paid directly after using the magical power, through diminished energy, an illness, or perhaps a loss of life itself.

The Hidden Force

Most systems of magic assume that there are two worlds. The first is the everyday world where material things, normal sensory experiences, and practical knowledge are the reality. The other is the supernatural world, a world in which a magical force is latent, or perhaps inside of all that exists, and the ability to access this mysterious power is extremely limited. Only a few select individuals, usually after first going through a lengthy initiation process, are able to gain access to this hidden power.

Magic's Moral Component

Magic itself is neutral. It is its application that makes it good or bad. Of course, if the hero uses magic for good purposes, then it is *white magic*. And if the villain and his or her wicked cohorts use magic to advance evil purposes, it is called *dark magic*.

White magic is used often for healing purposes, to help others improve in health, spirit, or well-being. White magic is usually an antidote to evil. Benevolent charms, bells, holy water, silver bullets, bracelets, rings, amulets, coins, and so on, are used as a form of white magic to overcome any dark magic that may be lurking.

Dark magic is often used for calling up evil spirits. A *necromancer,* often thought of as an evil magician, uses his magic for calling on the spirits of the dead.

Magical Words

If magic is going to be used, chances are that the perpetrators will need to know a few magical words. These spoken words, including spells, incantations, invocations, and enchantments, are all used to access the power of magic. In many stories, these phrases, which are chanted by the practitioner, can be found in spell books. Sometimes, the magical words must be used in combination with a particular ritual or rite.

Magical Tools

Every good magician has a few good tools at hand. A magician's tool can be just about anything. Some of the more common ones are listed here:

- Wands
- Cloaks
- Amulets
- Elixirs
- Charms
- Brooms
- Staffs
- Hats
- Orbs
- Swords
- Crystal balls

Practitioners of Magic

The trained mediums or practitioners of magic are often called *mages, wizards, witches, warlocks, necromancers,* and *sorcerers.* Sometimes practitioners come upon their magical powers accidentally. It is in their nature, and they have the special ability to access the force. Other times, a practitioner comes upon the secret knowledge and ability because a mentor, or teacher, of some sort, has passed it on. The young student, after having endured a precise, long, and arduous preparation period, develops the ability to use the magical powers.

Chapter Two

Threading the Theme

Fantasists, whether they use ancient archetypes of myth and legend or the younger ones of science and technology, may be talking as seriously as any sociologist—and a good deal more directly—about human life as it is lived, and as it might be lived, and as it ought to be lived. For after all, as great scientists have said and as all children know, it is above all by the imagination that we achieve perception, and compassion, and hope.

—Ursula K. Le Guin

Before our heroic student writers set off on this most challenging of storytelling endeavors, they must first know *why* they are departing. To understand why, they must begin with the end in mind. For in the journey's end, writers often find the reason they got started in the first place. This purpose for writing is the theme that the writer hopes to convey to the reader by the story's end.

Getting students to uncover a theme in an author's work is often a difficult goal. Getting them to decide upon, and actually incorporate, a theme in their own writing is even more complex. For some, it's a daunting task. Most students would rather skip all the deep thinking and questioning that accompanies the search for a theme, and simply jump into the writing of their stories. To prevent this mindless "jumping in," it is helpful to engage your students in a discussion about the purposes of writing.

As we teachers know, the main purpose of fiction is to entertain an audience. Fantasy in particular is often thought of as an entertaining form of escapism. While that may be true for most stories of fantasy, I like to tell my students that the very best works of fiction are those stories that not only entertain but also inform, educate, and even persuade. Yes, the best fiction does provide great entertainment, but it also exposes readers to new ideas and perceptions, teaches a thing or two, and persuades readers to think or act differently when it comes to a particular issue or circumstance. In other words, the best fiction has a transformational effect on readers; it changes them—ideally, for the better.

If a writer aspires to address all these aims in just one story, then she must have something important to say. This is the theme, the moral of the story, the deeper message the writer wishes to convey. So we begin our students' storytelling journey with the search for a theme. With a little luck, this theme, once found, will also serve to provide the motivation that our young student writer heroes will need to complete their long and difficult journey.

Thinking About the Theme

First, students need to be exposed to the concept of themes. You may be surprised by how little students understand story themes. It does, after all, require some abstract, formal-operative thinking. Students need to think and reflect on more than just the literal contents of the story to understand the theme. The following quick activity is designed to help students both understand the concept and get them thinking about the audience they will be addressing in their story. Once they know their audience, then they can start thinking about the message they would ultimately like to convey.

Understanding Basic Themes

In this activity students will be exposed to a few common themes. If they are having a hard time deciding on a theme to develop in their story, this activity should give them a few starting points. Of course, they are not obligated to incorporate any of these themes, but usually, no matter what theme they choose, it will most likely involve one of these basic issues.

Theme Thread: What Do You Have to Say?

Once you've introduced the concept of the theme and your students have had an opportunity to review a few common themes, pass out this worksheet, read it over, and give your students some time to reflect and think. Chances are that they will not come up with any particular big issue that they would like to address, but at least they will recognize that if they aspire to be extraordinary authors, they will have to have something worthy to say.

Additional Theme Threads

We all know that finding a theme is an arduous task. Some prominent writers will even attest to the fact that when they started out writing a particular piece they didn't have a clear idea about what the theme would be. Often, seasoned writers proclaim that the theme emerges as the writing progresses. Knowing that this is often true, additional opportunities throughout the journey are provided to help your students thread their theme. The first is found in the Theme Thread: Contrasting Characters activity in Chapter Five, "Crafting Your Characters." This minilesson encourages students to think about the inherent differences between the protagonist and the villain and how these contrasts can potentially point them to their theme.

Two additional activities that will help your students uncover a theme are found in the activities Theme Thread: Traveling Inward and Theme Thread: The Resolution in Chapter Six, "Plotting Your Path." In Traveling Inward, students first explore how to thread a story's theme by writing about the specific changes or learnings taking place in the mind and heart of their protagonist as he or she confronts challenges along the heroic path. And in The Resolution, students identify how the story's complications will be resolved in the ending. Take the time to teach these minilessons, and your students will be well on their way to effectively threading a theme throughout their growing narratives.

THINKING ABOUT THE THEME

We begin our story-writing journey with the search for something to say.

A story's theme is where you get to speak your piece. The theme is the moral of the story. It's the important message that you're hoping readers will take with them when they are finished reading. Themes attempt to tell a basic truth. But this basic truth should not be spelled out, explained, or stated in a clear and obvious way. If you do that, it will limit readers' interpretation of your story. Rather, your theme should be like a hidden thread woven deeply into the fabric of the story. The thread should show itself once in a while, but for the most part it should remain concealed so that the reader gets a feel for it by the story's end. You see, when writing your story you should try to have your own theme in mind, but you should also give your readers room to think and reflect, so that they can bring their own experience and insights into the reading. This will help get your readers thinking. If you're giving them something to think about, then you will draw them into the story. While they're there, with any luck, they will find your theme's thread, and eventually will come to hear your message.

Threading a theme is a difficult task. Sometimes, writers know exactly what they want to say. Other times, writers may not know their message until the writing begins. And sometimes still, the theme may not come to mind until the end, when the entire story has been told! However, if you start searching now for something important to say, then your theme *will* eventually make itself known. The important thing is to begin your writing with a desire to say something—say something that matters.

THE AUDIENCE

Who do you want to read your story? Every author writes with an audience in mind. What sort of reader will you be writing for? Who do you want to receive your message? Will it be grown-ups? Kids your age? Is your story more for girls or boys? Or is your story written for all audiences? Knowing your audience will help you to come up with something to say.

Take a moment to identify your audience:

_____

_____

UNDERSTANDING BASIC THEMES

OBSESSION WITH POWER

Power is one of fantasy's basic themes. It is an interesting theme. How do you think power should be used? Who has it? Who should have it? And once someone has it, how should they use it? If you choose power as your basic theme, then your story will show your readers your particular vision of the world. Your story will show them how you think the world should work, who should have the power, and how much power they should have. What do you think? Is someone being suppressed by the strong? Is someone misusing power and authority? Does it sometimes seem as though someone wants all the power and is willing to do almost anything to have it? Can you thread the theme of power throughout *your* story?

THE ENVIRONMENT

Fantasies are sometimes cast in a world that basically has two types of settings. The first is an evil empire in which the villain usually resides. In this domain, everything is hostile and scary, and often mechanized or artificial. The second is a paradise, where the hero typically lives. In this pastoral setting life is friendly, comfortable, natural. Nature even feels alive and conscious—trees talk, mountains move, rivers run.

Often tales of fantasy begin in the land of paradise, but once the action starts the hero or heroine and companions are cast out and forced to struggle with the hostile forces of a growing evil empire. Yet, somehow, the hero or heroine prevails and puts an end to the spread of the alienating force. The world then returns to its original, natural, pristine state.

Authors threading this theme often hope to remind us of the many environmental problems confronting us daily. They attempt to urge us to care for nature, defend it when it needs defending, and think beyond the interests of our own human species.

QUEST FOR IDENTITY

The quest-for-identity theme is closely related to the power theme. The quest for identity explores the relationship between an individual and the society in which he lives. Sometimes this relationship is expressed as a tug of war between societal norms and the individual. What do you think? Should the individual always get to decide? Or should society have a lot of decision-making power? Is there something that you can tell your readers about an individual's quest for identity?

UNDERSTANDING BASIC THEMES
(Continued)

SELF-RELIANCE

One of my main themes is self-reliance, the ability to compete against odds and to beat them. A lot of kids' books have somebody who learns to come to terms with some dreadful situation, and it's all about them continuing to suffer at the end of the book. I don't want to write "victim" books. I want a triumph, a hero or a heroine, and that's what I write about.

—Nancy Farmer
Locus: The Magazine of the Science Fiction and Fantasy Field

Nancy Farmer's *The House of the Scorpion* is about a boy named Matt who was harvested as a clone of the great El Patrón Alacrán. Matt's story begins with the old man's DNA, then moves on to a cell splitting inside a petri dish, an embryo, and fetus inside the womb of a cow, and finally, an animal caged in a room piled high with sawdust. Eventually, the resilient Matt learns that he is to be used for spare parts—to replace the used, worn-out parts of El Patrón, who is lord of the country Opium. Once Matt comes to terms with the circumstances surrounding his existence, he learns to rely on himself, overcomes the odds, and escapes from his horrible fate.

Writers addressing the self-reliance theme, like the quest-for-identity theme, are often writing a type of coming-of-age story. In these stories, protagonists go through a transformation: They get older, learn to rely on their own devices, and come to understand who they are. In the end, these heroes are also capable of identifying and being happy with their particular place in the world.

THEME THREAD:
WHAT DO YOU HAVE TO SAY?

Stories make us more alive, more human, more courageous, more loving. Why does anyone tell a story? It does indeed have something to do with faith, faith that the universe has meaning, that our little human lives are not irrelevant, that what we choose or say or do matters, matters cosmically.

—Madeleine L'Engle

What you say matters. It matters plenty. Probably much more than you know.

So tell us.

Tell us something important.

Tell us something that *really* matters.

Tell us something that could change the world.

What do you want people to know?

What do you think people should learn?

What do you want people to do?

What really gets under your skin?

If you could make people think, *really* think about something, what would you want them thinking about?

Would this thinking change their minds?

Inspire your readers.

Give them great joy.

Make them think about something that matters.

Make your story matter.

What is it that *you* have to say?

Chapter Three

Forming the Fantasyland

*A fantasy world is pure speculation, a map of
the human psyche labeled north, south, east,
west. But it is a true map, nonetheless, and no
one knows better than the traveler who uses that
particular map whether there really be dragons
where X marks the spot.*

—Jane Yolen

After contemplating a theme to thread through their
stories, students will next need to decide *where* their stories are
going to take place. To do this, they will need to create their very
own fantasylands; each child will need to make, shape, and construct a detailed map of a completely unique, personal, speculative
world.

Aside from the fact that kids love the freedom to use their
imaginations to create their own fantasylands, map making is also
a huge motivation for writing a story. For many students, making a map is key to the fun part of the writing; for some it's as if
they're creating their own special game board and they can't wait to
begin playing. And, as an added benefit, students are introduced
to three-quarter-perspective drawing. These are important tools
certain to aid any good fantasy writer. So just start with the map-
making prompt, and proceed through the map-making instructions
provided in this chapter, and your students will be well on their
way to forming their very own fantasylands.

The Fertile Crescent, from Book Two in *The Taylor Thomas Trilogy: The Rock of Jerusalem,* by Mr. Gust

Before my students commenced forming their fantasylands, I brought in and displayed a map that I had created of *the Fertile Crescent*. As I explained to my students, I produced this map for the second book of *The Taylor Thomas Trilogy: The Rock of Jerusalem,* which I had been busy working on at the time. My students were genuinely impressed and quite surprised that I, too, was working on writing a fantasy book, or trilogy, of my very own.

I explained that I formed this map by first drawing the continents and bodies of water. Then I drew in the mountains, rivers, and some of the towerlike structures called ziggurats that the Mesopotamians had erected in the area around 1787 BCE. After using colored pencils to add color, the map was then scanned onto watercolor paper and then painted to deepen the colors. Finally, I scanned the map again, and then had a graphic artist help me with the border and the burnt edges.

Mr. Gust's map of the Fertile Crescent, for the second book in *The Taylor Thomas Trilogy: The Rock of Jerusalem.*

It is incredibly motivating when I share with my students the fact that I myself have done the very same thing that I am now asking them to do. They pay much closer attention, and put in much more effort knowing that I walked through the fire first. So I urge you, fellow teachers, to find a way to set an example for your students to emulate.

Map-Making Assignment

Map making is an incredibly important step in the story creation process. As soon as students put their pencils to paper and start drawing, the story begins. First, all the little places of this new strange land start forming under their watchful eyes; the magical landscapes and mysterious terrain, the homes and villages, castles and caves, tree houses and subterranean kingdoms. Each student's map becomes a land where all sorts of interesting creatures and characters are born.

To begin, you will want to expose your students to a few classical maps found in any number of published fantasy books. Display the maps, study them, and point out the landscapes and a few choice locations of interest. This will help familiarize them with how it will be done for their own maps. And *please* don't forget to invite your students to read the books from whence the maps came!

Some examples of fantasy books containing excellent maps follow:

The Hobbit, by J.R.R. Tolkien

Eragon, by Christopher Paolini

Dragon Rider and *The Thief Lord*, by Cornelia Funke

The Chronicles of Narnia, by C. S. Lewis

The Spiderwick Chronicles, by Tony Diterlizzi and Holly Black

The Angel's Command, by Brian Jacques

Once they have gray, light brown, or white construction paper (18 inches by 24 inches) and colored pencils laid out before them on their desks, you may want to remind your class that they are about to create a world that *can* have a great effect on the thoughts and minds of others. So, they must be careful with the land their mind's imagination may form, for it has the power to wield the inner workings of their mind, as well as of another's. A short passage from Tolkien's essay "On Fairy-Stories" in his book *Tree and Leaf* helps clarify the enormity of the task at hand.

> The mind that thought of light, heavy, grey, yellow, still, swift, also conceived of magic that would make heavy things light and able to fly, turn grey lead into yellow gold, and the still rock into swift water. If it could do the one, it could do the other; it inevitably did both. When we take green from grass, blue from heaven, and red from blood, we have already an enchanter's power—upon one plane; and the desire to wield that power in the world external to our minds awakes.

So, a classroom of enchanters they become! They are joining an elite group. In the words of Tolkien, one of the world's greatest enchanters himself …

We may put a deadly green upon a man's face and produce a horror; we may make the rare and terrible blue moon to shine; or we may cause woods to spring with silver leaves and rams to wear fleeces of gold, and put hot fire into the belly of the cold worm. But in such "fantasy," as it is called, new form is made; Faerie begins; Man becomes a subcreator.

With a regular pencil in their little hands, it is now time to guide your budding "subcreators" and "enchanters" through the various steps of the map-making process as *you* also construct an example map on the board, butcher paper, or multimedia presentation. Just follow the steps provided in the student pages and have some fun.

Map-Making Prompt

To get your students started, first pass out the prompt, and read it over with the class. Promote a discussion that addresses the following questions:

- How can your fantasyland setting give birth to a cast of characters?
- What does it mean that your setting will pull your characters on an adventurous journey?
- How will a good fantasy setting create conflicts, hardships, and challenges for your characters to solve?
- How might the setting provide resources that will help your characters solve any number of problems you might put them through?

The intent of the discussion is to prompt your students' thinking about the possible "powers" that could be present in a fantasyland setting. With this magical thinking in mind, students will be ready to begin forming their fantasyland.

Forming the Land

With proper materials in hand, your students will first draw their map's border. Students will then draw the outline of the bodies of land, a beach with waves, and horizontal lines to add depth to the ocean's waters.

Character Domains

Before your students get too far into the process, they must remember to include places on their map for the hero's home, two places of conflict, and finally, the villain's domain.

Determining the Terrain

Next, your students will need to draw in their fantasyland's various terrains. Instruction is provided to help your students with drawing mountains, canyons, rivers, lakes, forests, deserts, and more.

Villages and Places

After students have drawn in the terrain, they will need to draw in the villages and the structures to be found there. They will also need to begin naming various key locations on their map.

Embellishing the Map

To complete the map, students may choose to draw a title scroll, a compass rose, some symbols or runes, and a distance or size scale. They will also need to burn the edges of their map to give it an antiquated feel.

De Janee Smith created this wonderful map of
"The Mystical Island."

Brianna Pamanes called her fantasyland "Flower Power."

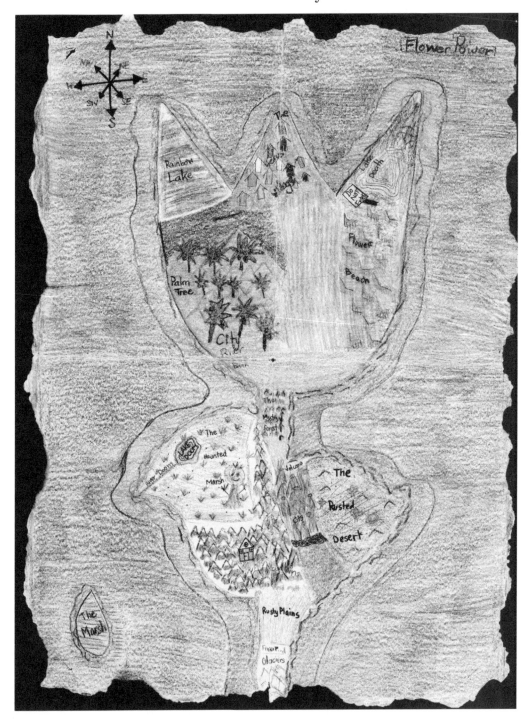

Shelem Celis designed the interesting "Emperor Island."

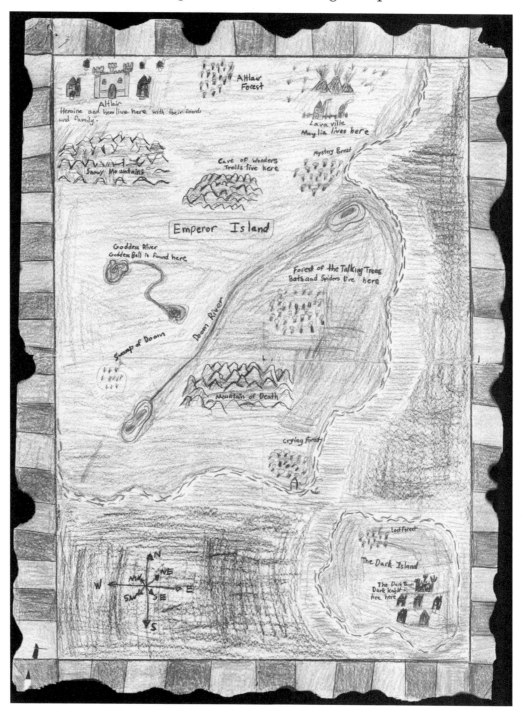

MAP-MAKING PROMPT

Any story ever written had to take place somewhere. In most fiction, the story is told in a setting within a "real" place and time. In fantasy, the writer has an opportunity to create a world anew. This is called *world building*.

When forming a fantasy world, the writer creates a unique land, which, if drawn clearly enough, will serve to pull the characters on an adventurous journey. A good fantasy setting creates conflicts, hardships, and challenges for characters to resolve. It may even provide resources that could help your characters solve any number of problems.

You'll need to focus on your map as much as you would a favorite character. In a way, your fantasyland is a character. But, unlike characters, fantasylands *usually* can't act. What they can do, however, is create moods, sights and sounds, smells and feelings, and possibly even certain tastes.

The first challenge in writing a fantasy story is to draw a map. You'll need to create your own fantasyland!

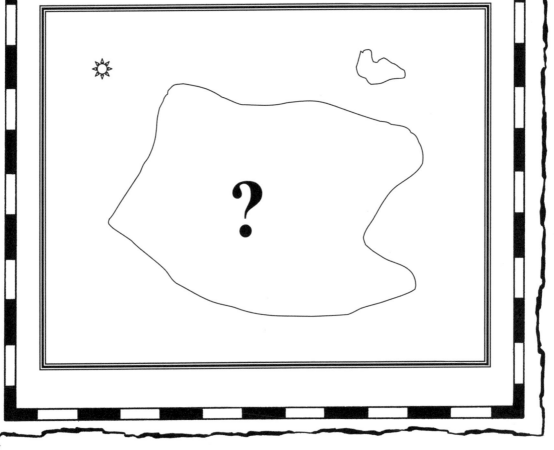

FORMING THE LAND

To get started, you're going to need a large piece of construction paper. In the old days, maps were made out of parchment. Parchment is a creamy, yellowish material that was made from dried and treated sheepskin, goatskin, or other type of animal hide. But we don't need to go that route in this day and age; a large piece of construction paper will do just fine.

Now, you'll need to draw a border. Most fantasyland maps have some sort of interesting border. Borders help make your map appear old or antiquated.

Forming the Fantasyland

Next, you'll want to draw an outline of your fantasyland. You could do this by drawing an irregular shape and call it an island. Or you might want to draw a curving coastline down the length of your paper. You may even want to draw the outline of an animal. Or better yet, try a "body of land." Map out your body—trace it—any part of it—and use that as your fantasyland.

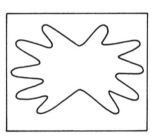 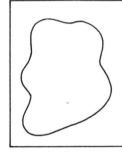 

After the border is drawn, the next step is to draw the beach and the waves that caress the land.

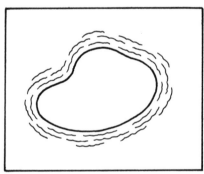

Finally, to give the ocean around the land some depth, draw horizontal lines that reach outward from the land toward the deepening sea.

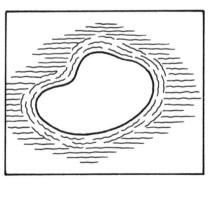

CHARACTER DOMAINS

Now you're almost ready to start forming your fantasyland. When creating your story's setting, you'll want to include lots of interesting places. Keep in mind, however, that a story will unfold on this fantasyland. In order for that to happen, your story's hero will need to go on a quest. He or she will need to travel to some faraway place. Therefore, your fantasyland should have each of the following:

HERO'S HOME

The hero or heroine has to live somewhere, right? Where do you think that character might live? Up on a hill? A mountaintop? A shaded valley? How about in a forest? Maybe even up in the trees? Will your hero live in a cozy home tucked into a hill? Next to a lake or river? Or perhaps in a subterranean kingdom? You'll think of something. This may also be the starting point for your hero's journey.

TWO PLACES OF CONFLICT

Next, you will need to create at least two other places of conflict. These will serve as settings where your story's hero will encounter a problem or two on the way to the grand and exciting climax.

VILLAIN'S DOMAIN

Finally, you should also consider the role of the evil place. This is the setting's version of the villain. If you didn't choose a forbidden forest, cold cave, desolate desert, soupy swamp, or menacing mountain for one of your places of conflict, you could consider using one for the villain's domain.

DETERMINING THE TERRAIN

Now that you have the borders of your fantasyland drawn, and you know what key locations need to go in it, you'll need to draw the land's terrain. If you need help with determining this terrain, here are some types to consider. If you don't know what a word means, and it's an interesting-sounding word, try looking it up. Like the word *butte*. Do you know what a butte is? How about a *knoll?* Or even an *abyss?* Uh-oh! You might not want to know what an abyss is.

island	cove	forest
peninsula	ocean	prairie
coastline	lake	beach
mountain	mesa	marsh
river	cliff	ravine
creek	canyon	delta
valley	plain	abyss
knoll	butte	cavern
hillside	swamp	gorge
volcano	everglade	desert
chain of islands	cave	summit
frozen tundra	pond	dunes
glacier		

Mountains

Canyon

DETERMINING THE TERRAIN
(Continued)

Forming the Fantasyland

VILLAGES AND PLACES

Now that you have determined your terrain, you'll need to create a few places where people and creatures will live.

LOCATIONS OF VILLAGES

So far you've heard that a hero and a villain should be in your story. And of course, there will be other characters in your story as well. These characters have to live somewhere, don't they? Well, will they live . . .

Near rivers or lakes?

In caves?

Under cliffs?

On the coastline?

In a valley?

On a mountaintop?

Elsewhere?

STRUCTURES BUILT

And what will your characters live in? To house these characters, structures need to be built. Will they live in . . .

Wood houses?

Grass huts?

Places of worship?

Castles?

Tree houses?

Caves?

Elsewhere?

VILLAGES AND PLACES
(Continued)

NAMING PLACES

Now that you have drawn the landscapes, villages, and a few structures, you'll need to name these places. One way to do this is to help make your fantasy settings come alive. It's like the various terrains have somehow taken on a life all their own! Here are just a couple of examples:

Gulping Gulch

Masticating Mountains (They're always chewing!)

Roaring River

Once you've decided on the names, carefully write them on your map in the appropriate places.

EMBELLISHING THE MAP

TITLE SCROLL

You've also got to give your fantasyland a name. For this, you'll want to draw a scroll for the title of your land somewhere on your map.

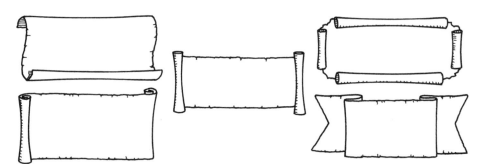

COMPASS ROSE

A compass rose identifies the cardinal directions (north, south, east, and west) with respect to the layout of your map. Most maps have north at the top. Make sure you include a compass rose somewhere on your map. Usually, the compass is placed somewhere in the middle of a large body of water.

SYMBOLS AND RUNES

Many maps have a legend of symbols. Some call these *runes,* but they are also known as *scripts, pictographs*, and *glyphs*. Maybe you'll want to create your own.

Adventures in Fantasy

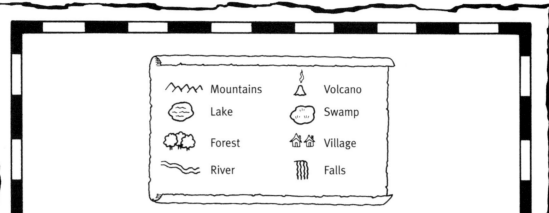

DISTANCE AND SIZE SCALE

You may want to provide a scale to indicate how long it would take to travel a certain distance on your map. Some maps have divisions in terms of weeks, others in length of days. You could also create a scale that simply shows distance in miles or leagues.

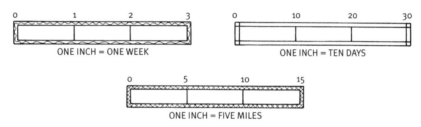

BURNT EDGES

As a finishing touch, you might want to burn the edges of your map. This will definitely give it an interesting feel and look. Be careful, though! And have an adult present, please.

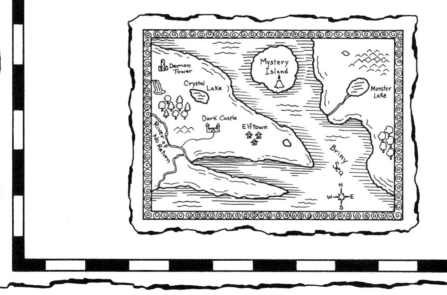

Forming the Fantasyland

Chapter Four

Setting the Surroundings

Saying that description and setting are important in fiction is like saying that an engine is important in a car. Other things are essential too, like a steering wheel and tires and dozens of other gizmos. The car won't do much without most of them. But it won't even start without an engine. Neither will your story really start until your reader is aware of the time and place.

—Ron Rozelle

After contemplating a theme to thread through their stories and forming their fantasyland maps, students will next need to set their story's surroundings. By describing their own fantasyland setting, students will also begin to build an arsenal of tools, weapons, and magical aids—or skills—that will be needed when the time comes for writing their stories.

Rarely do students spend the time *thinking* about a story's setting, much less describing it in a narrative. Therefore, to get students thinking, invite them to write a travelogue of their land. In this traveler's guide, they will be required to use plenty of sensory details and mood words to describe four key settings—the story's exposition, two places of conflict, and the villain's domain—and a combination of transitional expressions and action words to explain how to get there.

The training endured here, while setting the story's surroundings, will also serve your student writers later on, when it's time to describe the journey their story's hero or heroine will take to gain his or her reward. Our heroic student writers will come to realize how important it will be to avoid any *whiteout* that may otherwise develop in their stories. Whiteout is when the reader has no idea where the characters *are* any more. There's nothing but dialogue. Everything in the scene is white. Sometimes, there is no setting. And certainly, the reader isn't *in the scene* at all.

Riding Horseback Through a Storm on the Grasslands, from *Eragon*, by Christopher Paolini

Reading excerpts from books is a great way to provide wonderful examples of what we hope our students will attempt to approximate. This excerpt from *Eragon* not only provides a fabulous description of a setting but also tells us *exactly* what we are looking for in our students' writing.

In this part of the story, Eragon, a fifteen-year-old Dragon Rider boy, is meeting up with his horse Cadoc, and Brom, his wizardly helper. They are traveling across the grasslands on their way to the village Yazuac that sits on the shore of the Ninor River in the land called Alagaësia. A storm has come upon them. Eragon is dismounting his blue dragon Saphira, and joining his horse and helper.

> Eragon shook his head and dismounted. Cadoc trotted over to him, nickering. As he stroked the horse's long cheek, Brom pointed at a dark curtain of rain sweeping toward them in rippling gray sheets. "What else?" cried Eragon, pulling his clothes tighter. He winced as the torrent reached them. The stinging rain was cold as ice; before long they were drenched and shivering.
>
> Lightning lanced through the sky, flickering in and out of existence. Mile-high blue bolts streaked across the horizon, followed by peals of thunder that shook the ground below. It was beautiful, but dangerously so. Here and there, grass fires were ignited by strikes, only to be extinguished by the rain.
>
> The wild elements were slow to abate, but as the day passed, they wandered elsewhere. Once again the sky was revealed, and the setting sun glowed with brilliance. As beams of light tinted the clouds with blazing colors, everything gained a sharp contrast: brightly lit on one side, deeply shadowed on the other. Objects had a unique sense of mass; grass stalks seemed sturdy as marble pillars. Ordinary things took on an unearthly beauty; Eragon felt as if he were sitting inside a painting.

Feeling as though we are sitting inside a painting is exactly what we writers are shooting for. For me, Christopher Paolini, who was fifteen years old when this piece was written, certainly accomplished that task.

After reading a piece like this to your students, it helps to explore the writing, looking for colorful adjectives, active verbs, mood words or phrases, characters' thoughts, feelings and movements, metaphors, and similes. Fortunately, Paolini's three short paragraphs provide ample opportunity to study each of those literary elements.

Landing in a Valley near the Great River, from *The Chronicles of Narnia: The Magician's Nephew*, by C. S. Lewis

In the chapter titled "Strawberry's Adventure," Digory is with Polly riding on the back of a winged horse named Fledge. The horse's name used to be Strawberry, but Aslan the lion gave the ordinary horse a pair of wings and ordained him to be "father of all flying horses." Digory, Polly, and Fledge are on a journey searching for a tree growing in the middle of a garden on a steep green hill, near a blue lake, surrounded by mountains of ice. Digory's job is to pick an apple from the tree and bring it back to Aslan. Little does Digory know that the apple is going to cure his ailing mother's illness. Later, after Digory plants the apple's core, the seeds within will grow into an enormous tree that will provide all the needed lumber for the wardrobe that Digory will later make as a grown man.

> So Fledge came lower and lower. As they came down nearer to the earth and among the hills, the air grew warmer and after traveling so many hours with nothing to listen to but the beat of Fledge's wings, it was nice to hear the homely and earthy noises again—the chatter of the river on its stony bed and the creaking of trees in the light wind. A warm, good smell of sun-baked earth and grass and flowers came up to them. At last Fledge alighted. Digory rolled off and helped Polly to dismount. Both were glad to stretch their stiff legs.

I chose this short excerpt from *The Magician's Nephew* because of Lewis's attention to the senses of touch, smell, and hearing. Again, we also attempt to determine what words are used to set the mood of the place: "air grew warmer," "nice to hear," "homely," "earthy," "chatter," "warm, good smell," "sun-baked," "came up to them."

Daybreak on a Mountain and in a Meadow at Noon, from *The Temple of Light*, by Mr. Gust

For ages, writing teachers have been urging teachers to share their own writing with students. Doing so, they say, will expose students to the struggles they themselves went through to produce a piece, even something as simple as a description of a setting. Taking the experts' advice, I did as suggested, and read to my students a bit of my work.

I was actually quite nervous before starting. So I prefaced my reading with a warning to my students to go easy on me if they really didn't like it. Plus, I certainly didn't want to torture them with the chore of having to listen, and pretend they liked it, if it wasn't any good. So they could stop me—but stop me gently—if their ears started hurting. In spite of my reservations, I read my work, and much to my surprise, it was a big hit. They loved it. *Or so they said*, I thought, to myself privately.

I questioned them: "Ah, you're just saying that. Because if I'm reading all you have to do is sit there and listen, right? That's not *working* very much. You're all just looking to get out of doing your own writing. Aren't you?"

Two boys, Michael and Chijioke, argued the strongest for me to keep reading. Both were notorious for trying to get out of writing. Yet they were smart, likeable fellows. And they both had huge, charming smiles that they flashed often.

So after their prodding I kept reading. But only for a while. After a few minutes, the nagging feeling that I ought to get the kids back on task crept up my spine. I put aside the typed pages, and continued with the plans for our day.

For days, Michael and Chijioke—the classroom's two most rambunctious boys—continued to urge me to read more of my story. I declined their gracious offer, still not exactly sure if their compliments were sincere. Those two were a couple of connivers, and I knew it. I wasn't going to let their compliments fool me. I knew what they were up to. Trouble was, I didn't. Later, at the end of the year, while we were picnicking in the park, celebrating our culmination—my students were fifth graders, and moving on to middle school—I asked Michael and Chijioke if they were telling the truth when they told me they liked my writing, and wanted me to read more. Turns out, I was wrong. They really did like it, and they really wanted me to read more.

Those comments alone made me glad I read the passage. And I know it made my students try all that much harder, especially after I explained how much work I had put into writing these four paragraphs. I spent hours researching the flora and fauna of this particular mountain, and learning about the various myths told about it as well. I even told them about the trip I took to the mountain and the meadow that I attempt to describe. I know they were impressed. And I'm certain it heightened their writing efforts as a result.

What follows is a small sample of the writing that I shared with my students. I was hoping it would provide yet another example of what to look for in a setting description. It's an excerpt from the first book in the Taylor Thomas Trilogy that I was working on at the time. In this first book, *The Temple of Light*, the sixteen-year-old protagonist, Taylor Thomas, awakes at sunrise on the side of a magical mountain. Her helper, Zanadar, a Pleiadian alien, had only just transported her there, the night before, from her home in Los Angeles. In this excerpt, Taylor is on the mountainside, searching for the threshold, so she can get through the portal, and under the mountain to the subterranean city that lay within.

The next morning, Taylor was awakened by the buzz of a hummingbird hovering directly over the opening of her little cave. At first, she thought it was her alarm clock back home, and that the events of last night were just a dream. She opened her eyes half expecting to see her bedroom, but then realized that that wasn't the case at all. She was freezing and shivering so hard that she found it difficult to breathe. After a few forced inhalations, she climbed out from under the rock, stood up stiffly, and stretched. While trying to rub some heat into her cold muscles and bones, she looked around at her surroundings.

Last night Taylor didn't have much of a chance to survey the area; but this morning, with the aid of the sun's light, she could see that the mountain was full of life.

Adventures in Fantasy

All around her chipmunks darted about, searching for food. Higher up the mountain she could hear a woodpecker hammering on a tree. Directly overhead, a bird with a brilliant blue body and charcoal-colored, crested head, dark eyes, and pointy beak was flying from tree to tree. Higher in the sky, circling above the tall ponderosa pines looking for a meal below, a hawk displayed its regal wingspan. And, with no warning at all, a bird sporting a fat white belly, white forehead and face, and dark gray back and tail, swooped over Taylor's right shoulder, coming within inches from her ear.

By noon she had climbed much higher on the mountain. The alpine forest had thinned and Taylor was now in a lush meadow near the timberline. The meadow's soft, moist ground was laced with trickling streams veiled by long grasses hanging over the banks. Springs from above were saturating the soil, providing a stable home for a variety of herbs, rushes, grasses, and flowers. Taylor enjoyed walking on the spongy grass so much that she took off her shoes and socks and bounced around a bit. The cool grass felt particularly refreshing on her now hot, steaming toes. She was very careful, however, not to step on any of the prettier mountain heather, alpine laurel, and arnica shrubs that were growing nearby. She admired the delicate purple, yellow, and red flowers they offered and wanted to make certain that she did nothing to disturb them.

The sun was high in the sky and the temperature was getting hot, so Taylor decided she would stop for a while to rest, cool down, and enjoy her surroundings. By now she was extremely thirsty, so she knelt down at the edge of a gurgling stream, and cupped her hands together. When she lowered them into the icy, lucent water, a strange, energizing current passed through her arms and into her body. "Whoa!" she said out loud, as a tingling sensation ran up and down her spine.

One of the tales told regarding this particular mountain is that it offers water that has special powers. And as we all know, waters with special powers are common in stories of fantasy. Take *The Hobbit*, for example. Remember how Bilbo and the dwarfs were warned by Beorn not to drink from or bathe in the enchanted stream that crossed the path running through Mirkwood Forest?

The Travelogue Assignment

Now that students have completed their maps, it's time for them to write a travelogue of their fantasylands. In this assignment, students will use sensory, mood, transition, and action words to describe four key locations on their maps. Hence, the goal of this assignment is for students to take readers into their new world. But once there, they must guide their readers on a journey to the land's most important locations. The more thoroughly students are able to describe these key settings in this travelogue, the better and more detailed the descriptions will be in their story. To complete this assignment, ask your student writers to take their readers from the hero's home, to two places of conflict, and finally to the villain's domain.

The writing prompt, guiding outline, rubric, and reader response pages should *always* be distributed to students *before* they begin the assignment. This

will help them acquire a clear vision of the final product. After everyone is aware of what is required of them, and headed in the right direction, then have your students complete the various activities, or minilessons provided (sensory and mood words, transitional expressions, and so on) to help them successfully reach their destination: the final product, or completed travelogue.

Travelogue Prompt

The prompt is to get your students psyched, motivated, and of course, clear on their direction. The map on the reproducible student page is sure to help make the task easier to visualize. Pass this page out first, read it over with your students, and make sure they are clear on the assignment's directions.

Travelogue Guiding Outline

After you read through the prompt, and before your students begin their rough draft of the setting description, you can offer the example outline provided if you believe it would be helpful for your young writers to have it to guide their work. You'll notice that the outline reminds students to use ...

- Sensory details and phrases with plenty of colorful adjectives
- Transition and action words to describe the direction that needs to be taken for readers to get from one location to another
- Mood words

Travelogue Rubric

If you'd prefer not to provide students with the guiding outline, it is always helpful to review the rubric by which their travelogues will be evaluated. This will make students aware of the specific criteria or objectives they must address in their writing. Before they begin their rough draft, read the rubric in class, discuss its contents, have students highlight or circle key phrases, and challenge them to set a goal for the score they would like to achieve.

Travelogue Reader Response

Writers need an audience for their work. Having an audience will inspire students to work harder. It also makes the writing more fun. Before students start their rough drafts, pass out copies of the Travelogue Reader Response. Read and discuss this page with your students. Then explain that after they have completed their rough drafts, but before they begin their revision process, they will need to have their travelogue read by at least three peer readers. When the time comes, set aside a large block of writing workshop time for students so that they can find peers they feel comfortable with. Have them exchange travelogues and be sure to guide the student readers to write appropriate responses in the spaces provided. Once the readers have responded, then have the writers read over the comments, consult with the respondents if necessary, return to their desks, think over what changes they would like to make, and then proceed to revise their work.

Using Sensory Words

After your students have been given the prompt, guiding outline, rubric, and reader response pages, but before they begin their travelogues, they might need a chance to pack a few more sensory words into their vocabulary bank. They'll need these words to describe the four key parts of their setting. To get the whole process started, you may want to provide a short list of sensory words. This quick flash of words is simply a way to get their brains going. Once they've read through the list, have students get together with a partner or two, and challenge them to add a few more of their own sensory words to the list. If they need help, they can always consult a thesaurus or dictionary if necessary.

Creating Sensory Phrases

With a few more sensory words packed into their vocabulary, students are finally ready to begin describing their setting. One way to start is to ask students to identify the objects that may be found in any one particular location. The next step is to take those objects and place at least two descriptive adjectives in front of them to construct a phrase. This phrase construction gives students an opportunity to brainstorm and stretch their minds to create accurate, colorful, sensory descriptions.

Setting the Mood

With sensory phrases compiled, it is now time to direct students to consider the mood of the place. Mood is a powerful and useful tool for a writer.

One very effective way of evoking a mood is to make good use of the setting. The place where a scene is set can echo the feelings of the character or reflect the atmosphere of the story. When writing fantasy, because of its invented settings and imaginary worlds, writers have a special task to make sure all aspects of the setting make sense.

For this activity, first ask students to think of a mood—any mood—that a setting might project. Take a few responses, then choose one particular mood word to work with. Write this mood word on the board. Then ask students to think of a setting that might naturally evoke this mood. Write that setting on the board as well. Finally, ask students to describe what might be seen, heard, felt, smelled, or tasted in this particular setting to give it that mood. Write these responses on the board. Then play with the responses provided: Ask your students to put together a few phrases to create a sample paragraph that could describe the mood or feeling of that particular setting.

Once students have been guided through this example, pass out the reproducible student pages, read through the introduction, and have students choose one or several mood words for each of their four settings. Then have them describe what their characters will encounter in that moody place.

Traveling the Transition Trail

One more step before students start writing their travelogues: They will need to think about how to link together the paragraphs that describe each separate

place. They need to do this to show the reader how to travel from one location to another. An excellent way to help your students do this is to provide them with a treasure chest of transition words: a prize the student writer heroes will acquire while helping readers travel the trail through their fantasylands.

First, read through the worksheet provided. Review the transition words (order by location words) and sample sentence starters. Then invite students to choose the transitions they might use to link together their paragraphs. Have them circle the transition words they think will work best. While writing their travelogues, students can refer back to this page, if needed.

Keeping the Action Moving

Another way to help your students link together paragraphs in this multiparagraph descriptive essay is to incorporate a variety of action words. Action words can help set automatically the readers' minds in motion so that they are looking ahead to the next destination.

First, read through the worksheet provided. Review the various action words offered, and make sure to go over the examples of how to start a sentence using these words. Then invite your students to choose an action word or two that they might use to link together their paragraphs. Have them circle the action words they think will work best. While writing their travelogues, if needed, students can also refer back to this page.

Setting Description Practice

With the new sensory and mood words packed into their vocabulary bank, if you feel students need a bit of practice describing a setting or two—or three, or more—eight setting examples are provided. Have students work independently if you like, or in pairs or teams, whichever is most productive and fun. Using as many sensory and mood words as possible, have your students describe each setting with as much detail as they can imagine.

TRAVELOGUE PROMPT

Now that you have completed your map, it's time to create a travelogue of your land. In this writing assignment, you will describe four key locations on your map. This will be a guide for readers so that they may explore your fantasyland.

Any good author must be able to effectively use sensory and mood words to describe a setting. Therefore, the goal of this assignment is to take readers into your world … and make your fantasyland come alive! But once there, you must use key transition and action words to guide readers on a journey to your land's most important locations. The more thoroughly you are able to describe these key locations, and explain how to get there, the better you will be able to do so in your story.

To complete this assignment, you'll need to take your readers from the hero's home to two places of conflict, and finally, to the villain's domain.

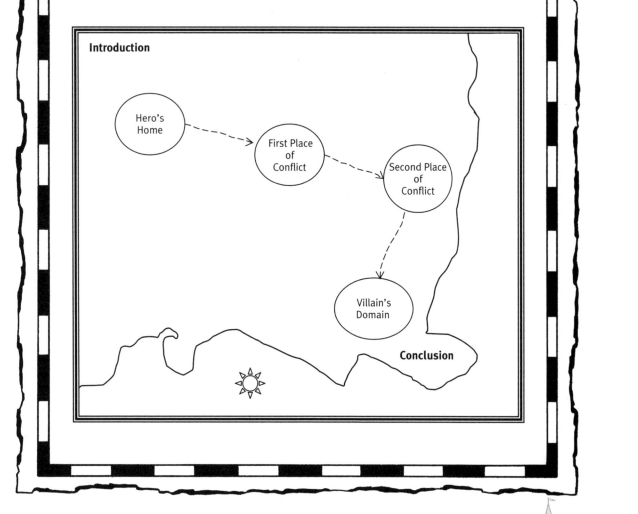

TRAVELOGUE GUIDING OUTLINE

I. Introduction
- Provide the name of your fantasyland.
- Write something general about the landscapes found on your map.
- Briefly describe the four different locations (hero's home, two places of conflict, and villain's domain). If you have names for these locations, mention them here.

II. Hero's Home
- Describe the location of the hero's home on the map.
- Provide sensory details and use phrases with plenty of colorful adjectives.
- Use mood words.
- Make us feel as though we are there!

III. First Place of Conflict
- Describe the direction taken from the hero's home to arrive at this location on the map using transition and/or action words.
- Provide sensory details and use phrases with plenty of colorful adjectives.
- Use mood words.
- Make us feel as though we are there!

IV. Second Place of Conflict
- Describe the direction taken from the first place of conflict to arrive at this location on the map using transition and/or action words.
- Provide sensory details and use phrases with plenty of colorful adjectives.
- Use mood words.
- Make us feel as though we are there!

TRAVELOGUE GUIDING OUTLINE
(Continued)

V. Villain's Domain

- Describe the direction taken from the second place of conflict to arrive at this location on the map using transition and/or action words.
- Provide sensory details and use phrases with plenty of colorful adjectives.
- Use mood words.
- Make us feel as though we are there!

VI. Conclusion

- Tell us what you told us (summarize).
- Tell us something suspenseful that will make readers want to "stay tuned" for the story yet to come.

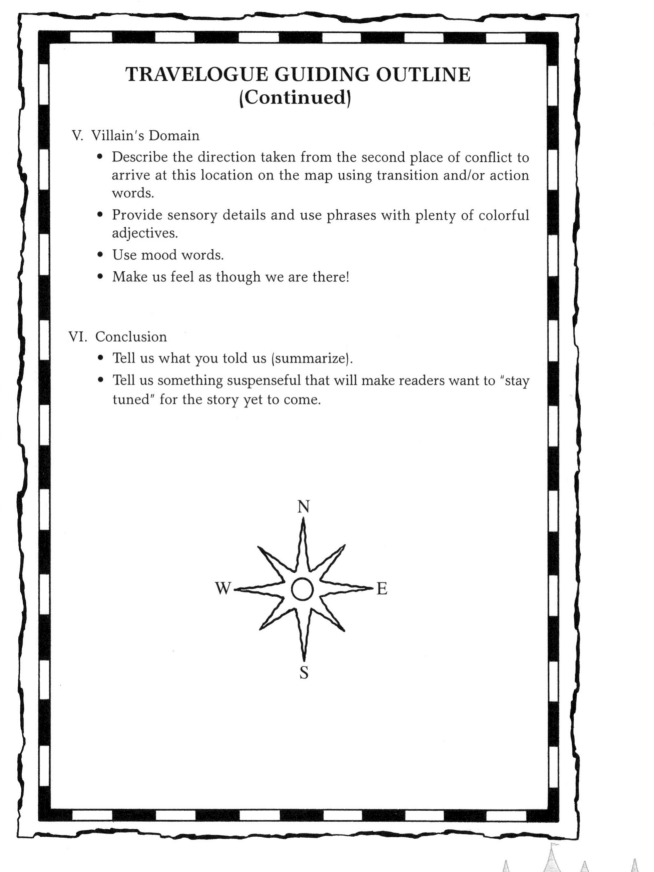

TRAVELOGUE RUBRIC

Goal/Score	Writing Strategies and Applications	Writing Conventions
4	• Expository composition vividly describes the setting using a wide variety of precise, colorful adjectives (sensory details) and mood words. The setting description makes the readers feel as though they are a part of the scene. • Provides a wide variety of transitional expressions that effectively link one paragraph to another in a clear line of thought. • Setting description shows not only revision but also incorporation of reader response comments. • Manuscript has been thoroughly edited and revised to improve the meaning and focus of the writing.	• Writing contains few, if any, errors in grammar, punctuation, capitalization, spelling, and sentence structure. • The errors do not interfere with the reader's understanding of the writing.
3	• Expository composition clearly describes the setting using a variety of colorful adjectives (sensory details) and mood words. The setting description paints a clear visual image in the mind of the reader. • Provides an adequate amount of transitional expressions to effectively link one paragraph to another in a clear line of thought. • Much or most of the editing and revising of the manuscript has been done to improve the meaning and focus of the writing.	• Writing contains some errors in the grammar, punctuation, capitalization, spelling, and sentence structure. • The errors do not interfere with the reader's understanding of the writing.

Goal/Score	Writing Strategies and Applications	Writing Conventions
2	• Expository composition vaguely describes the setting using some precise, colorful adjectives (sensory details) and mood words. The setting description paints a hazy visual image in the mind of the reader. • Provides some transitional expressions that link one paragraph to another in a clear line of thought. • Some editing and revising of the manuscript has been completed.	• Writing contains several errors in grammar, punctuation, capitalization, spelling, and sentence structure. • The errors may interfere with the reader's understanding of the writing.
1	• Expository composition fails to adequately describe the setting using little or no precise, colorful adjectives (sensory details) or mood words. The setting description makes the reader feel as though they are in an empty, white room (the "whiteout effect") • Little or no transitional expressions are used to link one paragraph to another in a clear line of thought. • Little or no editing or revising has been done to the manuscript to improve the meaning and focus of the writing.	• Writing contains numerous errors in grammar, punctuation, capitalization, spelling, and sentence structure. • The errors interfere with the reader's understanding of the writing.

Setting the Surroundings

TRAVELOGUE READER RESPONSE

Readers should keep in mind that the response page should provide the writer with a balance of compliments that encourage and delicately worded suggestions for improvement. After reading a peer's travelogue, readers should write comments that reflect on the following qualities:

- Does the author use a wide variety of precise, colorful adjectives, sensory details, and mood words?
- Does the description make you feel as though you are part of the scene?
- Does the author help you keep track of where each new setting is located on the map? Does the author help you go along on a journey through the story's fantasyland?
- Does the author use a *variety* of transitional expressions that link one paragraph to another in a clear line of thought?
- Does the author provide an introductory paragraph to get you started, and a concluding paragraph to summarize and lure you into reading the story?

Name of Reader 1: _____

Comments: _____

_____

_____

_____

_____

Name of Reader 2: _____

Comments: _____

_____

_____

_____

_____

Name of Reader 3: _____

Comments: _____

_____

_____

_____

_____

Adventures in Fantasy

USING SENSORY WORDS

Now we're going to expand our use of imagery to describe various locations on your map. *Imagery* is the ability to use sensory words to create a mental picture in the mind of the reader. Your goal is to make readers feel as if they are in the scene. The best way to do this is to include as many of the five senses in your setting description as possible. Good writers use sensory words to create strong images in the reader's mind. Here are some examples of sensory words you may wish to include in the description of your fantasyland's four key settings:

Sights: red, bright, dusty, sudsy, twisted, twinkling, murky, wiggly, wooden, pointed, green, clean, sparkling, cloudy, large, slender, pale, dark, black, shiny, metallic, hazy, glowing, dingy, flickering, shallow, deep, square, tall, swaying, bulky, glaring, grotesque, brilliant, glistening, shimmering, gleaming, radiant, towering, crooked, curved, gigantic, flashing, colorful, flaming, dazzling, foggy, sunny, starry . . .

Now add a few of your own: _____

_____

_____

_____

Sounds: booming, chiming, whispering, wheezing, moaning, gurgling, bubbling, cracking, clanging, hooting, rattling, screeching, clanking, rustling, tinkling, blasting, babbling, thumping, clinking, crunching, screaming, growling, barking, meowing, sputtering, tweeting, crinkling, hissing, thudding, buzzing, squeaking, sizzling, blaring, swishing, pitter-pattering, roaring, rumbling, howling, echoing, exploding . . .

Now add a few of your own: _____

_____

_____

_____

USING SENSORY WORDS
(Continued)

Smells and odors: flowery, dank, rotten, sweet, fragrant, sour, foul, fresh, aromatic, peppery, rusty, reeking, gingery, spicy, stagnant, perfumed, soapy, musty, evergreen, metallic, old, brand-new, salty, pungent, meaty, smoky, clean, moldy, stale, earthy, piney, antiseptic, putrid, medicinal . . .

Now add a few of your own: _____

_____

_____

_____

Tastes: salty, fruity, peppery, garlicky, bitter, burnt, flavorful, buttery, ice cold, juicy, bland, spicy, sweet, sour, cheesy, spoiled, tangy, greasy, rotten, delicious, yummy, creamy, chocolaty, biting, crisp, fishy, gingery, savory, nutty, minty, tart, sugary, hot, oily, mild, bittersweet, hearty, waxy . . .

Now add a few of your own: _____

_____

_____

_____

Touch, feelings in the air, and weather: sandy, fuzzy, gooey, icy, windy, warm, oily, hard, rough, dusty, slimy, slippery, shaggy, sticky, damp, prickly, scratchy, dry, breezy, cuddly, crusty, sharp, dull, soft, itchy, balmy, stringy, bouncy, grimy, windy, bumpy, smooth, grainy, moist, satiny, sharp, wet, tickly, furry, rubbery, greasy, gritty, cool, downy, muddy, rippling, wispy, tepid, breezy, steamy, stormy, rainy, frosty, sunny, gusty . . .

Now add a few of your own: _____

_____

_____

_____

Adventures in Fantasy

CREATING SENSORY PHRASES

There are four places in your fantasyland that you need to describe: the hero's home, the villain's domain, and at least two other places where the hero will meet an unexpected obstacle, challenge, or foe. Now is the time to create a bunch of sensory phrases using at least two adjectives to describe a place, or various objects, or things (nouns) found in these four locations. For example:

Object: rocks *Adjectives:* sharp, slippery *Phrase:* sharp, slippery rocks

Objects	Adjectives and Phrases
Hero's home:	Adjectives (sensory words):
Objects or things (nouns) found there:	Phrases:
First place of conflict:	Adjectives (sensory words):
Objects or things (nouns) found there:	Phrases:
Second place of conflict:	Adjectives (sensory words):
Objects or things (nouns) found there:	Phrases:
Villain's domain:	Adjectives (sensory words):
Objects or things (nouns) found there:	Phrases:

SETTING THE MOOD

Have you ever been in a place and all of a sudden found yourself in a certain mood? What about a dark forest, for example? Does that sound scary to you? Or how about in a small boat floating aimlessly on a rough ocean? Perhaps a little menacing? How about standing on the pinnacle of a snow-covered mountain? Chilling, maybe?

This feeling about a particular place is called *mood*. One way to evoke a particular mood for a setting is to think of that place as an active character. A setting can have a character or a mood of its own! Unlike human or animal characters, however, places *usually* can't act directly. The writer has to create influences and effects that are reflected in what the characters see, feel, and fear in its presence. For example, mysterious lighting, sound cues, temperature changes, or a smell wafting in the wind can help draw in the reader's attention. It can also create the suspicion that something is about to happen.

A place and the mood it projects can also help readers get to know the character who lives in that place a little better. For example, how you describe a hero's home could give the reader a sense of that hero's personality even before being introduced to the character.

Use the following mood words, or think of a few of your own, to apply to each of your four settings. Then describe exactly what you would see, hear, smell, taste, or feel in that place to give it that particular mood.

MOOD WORDS

chilling	scary	warm	cozy	gloomy
menacing	grim	dismal	light	lofty
angry	dark	calm	chaotic	airy
dank	breezy	heavy	dreary	soothing
eerie	still	desolate	despairing	carefree
melancholy	sad	unnerving	empty	happy
bleak	creepy	friendly	peaceful	frightful
comfy	bright	sinister	damp	cold
stark	forbidding	wretched	pleasant	cheerful
lovely	tranquil	fresh	murky	grave

SETTING THE MOOD
(Continued)

Mood of the
hero's home:

Describe what gives the hero's
home this mood:

Mood of the first
place of conflict:

Describe what gives the first
place of conflict this mood:

Mood of the second
place of conflict:

Describe what gives the second
place of conflict this mood:

Mood of the
villain's domain:

Describe what gives the villain's
domain this mood:

TRAVELING THE TRANSITION TRAIL

In the travelogue, you will need to direct your readers on a trail. They will need to know which way they have to go when moving from place to place. You can do this simply by using a variety of transition words. Transition words provide detailed expressions that link one paragraph to another in a clear line of thought. When you take your readers from one landmark on your map to another, it is important to help them follow along. Using transition words will help your readers move smoothly from one location to the next. Transition words will also make your writing more clear and accurate. Here are some terrific techniques for helping your readers travel the transition trail.

ORDER BY LOCATION WORDS

above	across	against	along	among	around
behind	below	beneath	beside	between	by
down	in	in back of	in front of	into	near
nearby	next to	off	on	on top of	outside
over	through	throughout	to the left	to the right	underneath
under	east of	west of	north of	south of	northwest
northeast	southwest	southeast			

Here are some examples of how to start a paragraph using order by location words:

Across the . . .

Northwest of _____ is the . . .

Under the . . .

To the south of . . .

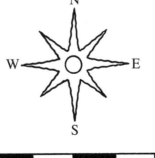

KEEPING THE ACTION MOVING

Another way to link paragraphs together to help the readers of your travelogue to follow along is to use action words. Action words can help set readers' minds in motion so that they are looking ahead to the next destination. You might want to try using one or more of these action words at the beginning of the first sentence of a new paragraph.

ACTION WORDS

traveling	moving	trekking	hiking	climbing	scaling
skipping	running	hopping	jumping	skiing	flying

Here are some examples of how to start a paragraph using action words:

Traveling south . . .

Moving southeast . . .

Trekking southward . . .

Hiking eastward across the _____ you will arrive at . . .

Climbing north over the mountains . . .

Scaling the cliff and heading west . . .

Crossing the desert . . .

Did you notice how in these sentence starters the order by location words were also used?

Finally, here is an example of how to start a paragraph with a sentence that uses both action words *and* order by location words:

Heading northwest you must travel over Menacing Mounts, through the Rambunctious River, and into the Formidable Forest.

SETTING DESCRIPTION PRACTICE

Everybody needs a little practice. Try describing these example settings before you describe your own. Include as many sensory and mood words as possible in your description.

Setting #1

> *What and where:* On the peak of a great mountain
> *When:* Middle of winter, late morning

_____

_____

_____

Setting #2

> *What and where:* In the middle of a dense forest
> *When:* Springtime, at dusk

_____

_____

_____

Setting #3

> *What and where:* On the muddy bank of a slow-moving creek
> *When:* Late summer, at midnight

_____

_____

_____

Setting #4

> *What and where:* On a small island in the middle of a large lake
> *When:* Early fall, at dawn

_____

_____

_____

SETTING DESCRIPTION PRACTICE
(Continued)

Setting #5

What and where: On the top of a sand dune

When: Middle of summer, high noon

_____

_____

_____

Setting #6

What and where: In an underground cavern

When: Would you even know when?

_____

_____

_____

Setting #7

What and where: At the edge of a deep canyon

When: Springtime, early morning

_____

_____

_____

Setting #8

What and where: The middle of a swamp

When: In the middle of summer, midday

_____

_____

_____

Chapter Five

Crafting the Characters

Beasts and birds and other creatures often talk like men in real fairy stories. In some part (often small) this marvel derives from one of the primal "desires" that lie near the heart of Faerie: the desire of men to hold communion with other living things.

—J.R.R. Tolkien

Now that your heroic student writers have determined *why* they've departed on this storytelling quest, and *where* the adventure will take place, they will next need to decide *who* will accompany them on the journey. It is time to create a clever cast of characters. To do so, your students must know a little something about the craft of characterization.

In order for students to begin developing their characters, they will need to know what type of characters exist. In most stories of fantasy, there are at least five general character types: the hero or heroine, the sidekick, the helper, the conflict character, and the villain. To prepare them to write their stories, you will ask your students to create a total of six characters. The number varies, of course, because in the real world, students are always negotiating, trying to include more or less characters in their stories. Based on needs and interests—or where they think their story is headed—it is up to you, the teacher, to help your students decide how many characters are appropriate for their stories.

Fantasy characters can come from just about anyplace. Sometimes a character can be crafted by actually using the raw materials supplied by the student's newfound fantasyland. Some creepy characters even climb right out of the ground! In this case, it's as if the writer is transformed into a sculptor and carves away at a mass of his land until the character he's looking for appears. Other times, characters can arrive on a student's fantasyland seemingly from someplace else. There are many types of fantasy characters and creatures, some of which students know all about, and others about which they may have no clue.

Contrasting Gandalf and Bilbo in *The Hobbit,* by J.R.R. Tolkien

To assist your students in the task of crafting a cast of interesting characters, you might also want to facilitate a study of *any* two characters in any work of fiction that you and your class are reading at the time. This activity is designed to help your students identify the differences between characters and explain how these differences contribute to the story's plot line. Story plot lines are moved along not just by the differences between the hero and villain, but sometimes because of the differences between any two related characters. For example, the differences between the hero and a sidekick could help move a story along. Sometimes sidekicks can provide some much-needed comic relief as they help to get the hero or heroine into all kinds of unanticipated trouble. Or, as in *The Hobbit,* the differences between the hero, Bilbo, and his helper, Gandalf, help move the plot along. Where would Bilbo be if not for Gandalf? After all, Gandalf is the one who gets Bilbo to go along on the journey to help the dwarfs get back their gold, isn't he? And who knows how many difficulties Gandalf gets Bilbo out of, anyway!

So, pass out the Character Contrast Table and Character Contrast Rubric, the first two worksheets in the following activity pages, and challenge your students to complete an essay that thoroughly describes the differences between two characters, while also identifying how this contrast contributes to the story's plot line. First, invite your students to fill in the boxes in the table as they identify the differences between two characters' actions, motives, appearance, thoughts, feelings, and so on. Then before they begin to write the character contrast essay, review the accompanying rubric. As always, make sure students know what is expected of them *before* they begin writing.

Introducing Zanadar from *The Temple of Light,* by Mr. Gust

I have always imagined the helper character to be the role we teachers play while accompanying our student writers' heroes on their adventures in fantasy. So to help my students with the task of creating their own unique cast of characters, and specifically their helper character, I like to share a bit of my own writing that I believe exposes the many possible forms a helper character may take.

Noel Parisi completed this character contrast of Gandalf and Bilbo from J.R.R. Tolkien's *The Hobbit*. Even though the two characters were both on the same "side," the contrast between the two did help move the story's plot along.

Noel
Parisi

Contrasting Characters ④

In The Hobbit, by J.R.R. Tolkien, there are two characters I will be contrasting. Their names are Bilbo Baggins and Gandalf the Grey. Bilbo is a hobbit while Gandolf is a wizard. They will both work together though, with thirteen dwarfs to get jewels.

Little do Bilbo Baggins is a quiet and patient person. He has very hairy feet. Bilbo wears no shoes because of his leathery feet. He is half the size of a human. Bilbo loves to wear bright colors like green and yellow. Bilbo has very long brown nails too. Bilbo is fat in the stomach. He has short brown hair. While Gandolf on the otherhand wears black imence boots. He has a long white beard. Gandolf always has his staff with him. He wears a grey cloak and a silver scarf. While Bilbo wore his hat, Gandolfs

In this short passage from my story, *The Temple of Light*, the character Zanadar introduces himself to Taylor, the young heroine. Zanadar is really an alien Pleiadian, Emissary of Light. But here, during his introduction, he is obviously searching for a way to describe himself so that Taylor will understand. When Zanadar appears, Taylor is in an educational store called Prophetic Learning Systems, where she is about to have her brain deconstructed by a bunch of nanobots; they are going to rebuild it so that it is better than before. She is about to cross the human-machine divide.

Waiting for her parents to complete the terms of the sale, Taylor makes her way to the back of the store. While there, she spins a globe in an effort to find the mountain she visited in an astral projected dream that she had the night before. When the globe stops, Taylor's finger is pointing directly at Mount Shasta in northern California, the mountain she really did visit in her dream:

"Ah! Sweet synchronicity!" said a deep, resonate voice from behind her.

Startled, Taylor swirled around to see who was there, invading her private moment. Someone or *something* was there, but whatever or whoever it was, was translucent and not at all a physical body. It was tall and violet with a little bit of yellow and green mixed in, as well. Each color in the figure blended together, yet stood apart. It looked like a man's physique, she thought, yet the color of it was more like light or energy. It certainly wasn't one of those nanobot swarm projections that created visual images of people. Taylor was familiar with those. "Who? ... What? ... are you?" she asked, while straining to see whatever it was.

"I am Zanadaaaarr the Avataaaaarrrr," the colorful personage boomed.

"Avatar? What's an avatar?" Taylor asked. Her eyes were open wide now, searching.

"I am the guide of souls," the booming voice continued, "the mysterious medicine man of hidden forest sanctuaries of trial and initiation. I am the master of the mythological realm, keeper of secret ways, speaker of words of potency. I am the one who appears and points to the shining sword that will slay the dragon. I am the helpful crone, the fairy godmother, the wise wizard, the merciful magician, and the valorous sorcerer." The voice paused for a moment, and then with great affect, belted out, "*I am the benign protecting power of destiny!*"

Later, when Zanadar's form finally does emerge, he appears as the stereotypical wizard common to many stories of fantasy. He envelops this outward appearance because he figures it is the only shape Taylor will truly comprehend.

By now, this Zanadar character was beginning to look more and more like a person. His physical body was taking form. He was a tall, old man with a long, gray beard. On this occasion, he was wearing a wizardly outfit: a long, purple robe and tall, pointed, purple hat. The hat had a wide brim that formed a long tail in the back. The hat's tail draped down the big man's long back. On his feet was a tall pair of enormous black boots.

And later still, after Taylor has been transported to the mountain, Zanadar, who had been sneaking up behind her, takes on yet another form: that of the Green Man, found in many tales of fantasy and fable:

The big old guy had discarded his purple wizardly wares and was now dressed in what was perhaps the best camouflage outfit anyone ever saw. Leaves and branches covered his entire body. In fact, he looked like a walking bush. Taylor could barely see his eyes because he was wearing a hat covered with leafy vines that concealed his broad face. "I was practically walking right beside you. You couldn't tell?" Zanadar folded his branchlike arms over his tree-trunk chest, obviously proud of his stealthy ways.

Thus, I expose students to my helper character, Zanadar, and his various physical forms to provide an example of what I would like them to emulate in their own writing. I find that it's a lot of fun, and quite an inspiration for my students as well.

Crafting a Cast of Characters Assignment

For this assignment, students will be asked to craft a cast of six unique and lively characters: the hero or heroine, a sidekick, a helper, two conflict characters, and a villain. The crafting, in this case, will require your student writer heroes to complete six comprehensive character descriptions.

To begin this assignment, as always, *first* distribute, read, and discuss the writing prompt, guiding outline, rubric, and reader response pages. Carrying out these activities will help students acquire a clear vision of the final product. After everyone is aware of what is required of them and headed in the right direction, have your students complete the various characterization activities provided that you deem necessary. This will help your students successfully reach their destination: the completed character descriptions.

You will definitely want to introduce your students to the various types of fantasy creatures and characters presented in this chapter. In addition, there are activities that will help students illustrate, name, or describe their characters' qualities, voices, and history, and more. Once these activities have been completed, make sure you give your students plenty of time for their imaginations to roam. Through learning this new craft of characterization, your student writer heroes will certainly have picked up a few more tools and "magical" literary aids to add to their growing arsenal of writing skills. It is a good thing, because they will need all the help they can get for the adventurous storytelling journey yet to come.

Character Description Prompt

There are basically two ways for students to write their character descriptions. The first is in the third person, whereby the author/narrator describes the various qualities of his or her created character. The other way is in the first person. In this approach, the character introduces himself or herself to the readers. Basically, these characters dictate to the writer what they would say, if they were really doing the talking. You wouldn't believe how much "character voice" this activity helps bring out. Pass out this page first, read it over with your students, and make sure they are clear on the assignment's directions.

Character Description Guiding Outline

Before beginning their rough draft of the character descriptions, if you believe that it would be helpful for your young writers to have an example outline to guide their work, you might want to offer the one provided. You'll notice that the outline reminds students to include each character's ...

- Contribution to the plot
- Appearance and actions
- Thoughts and feelings
- Strengths and weaknesses
- Personality traits and motives

Character Description Rubric

Before your students begin writing their rough drafts, make sure you distribute the rubric. Give everyone a copy, read it over, and discuss the various criteria listed. Once they all understand the requirements, have them pick the score they'd like to achieve. Then proceed through the series of activities and minilessons provided before inviting students to begin writing their rough drafts.

Character Description Reader Response

Before any revising is started, pass out this reader response page. Read through it and point out how similar it is to the rubric. Then facilitate a writers' workshop whereby students seek out peer readers for comments. Once each writer has acquired at least three student reader responses, have students look over the comments, consult with the readers if necessary, and then have them begin the revising, editing, and proofreading process.

Types of Characters

Before students get started writing their character descriptions, it's best to give them a description of a few types of characters. These will be the character types they are being asked to create. They are also the major character types one can find in just about every kind of story. Read and discuss the character types with your class. Mention the characters that you can recall from the various stories you have read that fit into one of the molds. And ask students if they can remember any books or movies that have incorporated these character types. Certainly, they'll be able to think of a few.

Fantasy Characters and Creatures

More than likely, many of your students won't know all that much about fantasy characters and creatures. Therefore, you will want to use this guide to help your students learn more of the lore of these interesting fantasy beings. Maybe they'll gain a few ideas for a character that they'd like to create. However, students are not required to choose from only the character types listed here. Perhaps they have a few novel ideas of their own to use for crafting a character. This list is only provided as a prompt to get students' minds churning.

Character Illustrations

Before students even begin to describe a character and his or her traits, sometimes it helps if they spend some contemplative time drawing. Drawing a character, no matter how crude a sketch, always gets students thinking. It also helps make concrete the exact types of clothes, build, and physical traits a character possesses. The drawing also gets students thinking about how each character moves, and what the character thinks and says. In short, drawing a character helps writers explore a character from top to bottom and inside out. Students will need one character illustration sheet for each character they craft.

Naming Characters

In *The Language of the Night,* Ursula Le Guin explains how she created the names of her characters: "People often ask how I think of names in fantasies, and again I have to answer that I find them, I hear them. This is an important subject in this context. From that first story on, naming has been the essence of the art-magic as practiced in Earthsea." With names like Ged, Arha, Ogion, and even Kurremkarmerruk, one can't help but think that Le Guin must have traveled to another world to hear the names. And maybe she did! For when explaining how she named Ged (pronounced with a hard *g*) for the main character of her *Earthsea Cycle,* Le Guin writes, "I worked (in collaboration with a wizard named Ogion) for a long time trying to 'listen for' his name, and making certain it really was his name."

You might want to invite your students to have a conversation with one of the characters in their story, as Le Guin did. Tell them to pair up with a favorite character—maybe a helper in their story—and have a conversation with that character. Tell them to *listen* for the other characters' names. Give students time to sit still to practice this lost art-magic of contemplation.

Once, after a long period of "listening," one of my fifth-grade students named the villain in her story *Humon Gusliar* (humongous liar). We all loved that name. Ever since, we've always taken the time to play with character names. Sometimes we try to make names out of any kind of quality word. We try to pick a word that describes a quality or characteristic of that very character and then start playing with the words, listening to the sounds they make, until a name arises, and finally fits the character chosen. Try it. It's a lot of fun.

Character Qualities

As long as we're busy thinking about character qualities, it's now time to get serious. What exactly are these character qualities and how will they mesh together to give the students' characters depth and complexity? This is the objective of this activity. Read and discuss with your students the character qualities they will need to identify. Doing so will help them create characters that readers will want to know more about.

Character Description Graphic Organizer

With an understanding of the character qualities that they will need to identify for each of their characters, students can next get to work using the graphic organizer. This planning web will help students form the language they will eventually use for their character descriptions. Students will need one of these planning webs for each of their characters.

Personality Traits

At times students need a little help with their vocabulary of personality traits to assign to specific characters. Here is a helpful list of traits to share with your students. You might want to break students up into groups to compile a list of their own first. Ask them, what kind of personality traits could a character in a fantasy story have? Think about the different kind of characters (hero, sidekick, helper, conflict characters, and villain) and start firing away.

Character Actions: How Do They Move?

Some students have a tendency to write dialogue as if nobody were moving or doing ... anything. Everybody's just standing there talking. One voice after another talk, talk, talking. Help your students make their characters move, scratch, blink, frown ... something. Characters have to be moving. And some characters move in particularly interesting ways. How characters move, slouch, slink, lean, and so on, says much about their personality, moods, feelings, and even thoughts.

Character History

This is an activity you will definitely want to have students complete for the main character. This is, after all, the character we will be following through-out the story. Most of the information compiled in this activity will probably never make it into the story. But knowing this much about the hero or heroine will help the writer to better understand how the character would react in just about any situation in which the writer might place the character.

Character Voices

Nothing is worse than having to read dialogue that sounds like it's not even coming from the character. Unfortunately, that's all too easy to do. This quick lesson offers an opportunity to get student writers to begin thinking and sounding like the character they are crafting. We don't want the writer's voice to blare through. What we want is to know how the character—no matter how wacky—will sound in the story. What types of moods does this character project? What crazy things might he say? Get your students' writing to reflect on each character's authentic voice.

Theme Thread: Contrasting Characters

Sometimes the difference between the hero and villain can reflect heavily upon the theme. This contrast, and the resulting struggle, is what fuels the story. Make sure your students take the time to contrast the various qualities of these two most important characters. While you're at it, have a brief discussion on how these differences could help thread a story's theme.

John Rivera, Mark Flores, and Ahmad Qashidi spread their character descriptions and illustrations on a table in preparation for reading and responding.

Francis De Guzman, Diego El Jechin, Nicole Jeter, and Ellen Kim are busy at work sharing and critiquing their characters.

Crafting the Characters

Tyler Nutsathitiya and Jor-el Leos review each other's character descriptions and illustrations.

CHARACTER CONTRAST TABLE

Title of book: _____

Character name:	Character name:
Role in the story:	Role in the story:
Actions:	Actions:
Motives:	Motives:
Appearance:	Appearance:
Thoughts and feelings:	Thoughts and feelings:
Personality traits:	Personality traits:

How do all these differences contribute to the plot of the story?

Crafting the Characters

CHARACTER CONTRAST RUBRIC

Goal/ Score	Writing Strategies and Applications	Writing Conventions
4	• The writing exhibits keenly perceptive reading comprehension skills and the ability to contrast two characters in a work of fiction and discuss the importance of this contrast to the plot of the story. • Important differences between the two characters are clearly and thoroughly described. • All thoughts or ideas are logically organized. • All statements about the differences are well supported or explained with facts and details from the story. • Writing shows not only revision but also incorporation of reader response comments. All of the editing and revising of the text has been done to improve the meaning and focus of the writing.	• Writing contains few, if any, errors in grammar, punctuation, capitalization, spelling, and sentence structure. • The errors do not interfere with the reader's understanding of the writing.
3	• The writing exhibits strong reading comprehension skills and the ability to contrast two characters in a work of fiction and discuss the importance of this contrast to the plot. • The differences between the two characters are clearly described. • Most thoughts or ideas are logically organized. • Most statements about the differences are supported or explained with facts and details from the story. • Much of the editing and revising of the text has been done to improve the meaning and focus of the writing.	• Writing contains some errors in grammar, punctuation, capitalization, spelling, and sentence structure. • The errors do not interfere with the reader's understanding of the writing.

CHARACTER CONTRAST RUBRIC
(Continued)

Goal/ Score	Writing Strategies and Applications	Writing Conventions
2	• The writing exhibits some reading comprehension skills and the ability to contrast two characters in a work of fiction and discuss the importance of this contrast to the plot. • Some of the differences between two characters are described. • Some thoughts or ideas are logically organized. • Some statements about the differences between the characters are supported or explained with facts and details from the story. • Some editing and revising of the text has been completed.	• Writing contains several errors in grammar, punctuation, capitalization, spelling, and sentence structure. • The errors may interfere with the reader's understanding of the writing.
1	• The writing exhibits little or no reading comprehension skills and the ability to contrast two characters in a work of fiction and discuss the importance of this contrast to the plot. • The differences between the two characters are not described or the descriptions are unclear. • Statements about the differences between the characters are not supported or explained with facts and details from the story. • Little or no editing or revising has been done to the text to improve the meaning and focus of the writing.	• Writing contains numerous errors in grammar, punctuation, capitalization, spelling, and sentence structure. • The errors interfere with the reader's understanding of the writing.

Crafting the Characters

CHARACTER DESCRIPTION PROMPT

The next step for creating your imaginary world is to give it some flesh and blood. From out of the ground of your fantasyland, characters must emerge: whole groups of people and creatures, heroes, villains, and more. It is time now to begin crafting your story's characters.

Basically, six different characters will be needed. Three of your characters will be considered the good guys, the other three ... well, of course, they're the bad guys.

Three Good Guys	Three Bad Guys
Hero or heroine	Villain
Sidekick	Two conflict characters or creatures
Helper	

It won't be easy to create characters worth reading about. To keep the reader engaged, your characters will need to be interesting and complex, different, maybe even strange. They must be ... *multidimensional!* In other words, they must contain many layers.

To write a complete description of *each* of your six characters, you can choose one of two different routes.

The first approach is to write a third-person description of your characters. In this approach, you'll be introducing your characters to an audience of readers.

The second approach is to allow your characters to do the introducing. That's right, if you take this second route, your characters will do the talking. If you choose this route you will be well on your way to helping your characters develop their own distinctive voices. Think: How would your characters describe themselves? See if you can take dictation from them as they tell you who they think they are and what life has been like lately. Your characters have to know what kind of personality they have, how they feel and think, how they look and move, and what kind of clothes they like to wear. They also need to know their strengths and weaknesses, and perhaps most importantly, what motivates them. All you have to do is to listen to your characters' voices and write it all down for them.

CHARACTER DESCRIPTION
GUIDING OUTLINE

Here is a sample outline of how each of your character descriptions might be organized:

I. Introduction
- Name
- Background information
- Where the character lives
- The character's contribution to the plot (hero, sidekick, helper, villain, or conflict character)

II. Looks, Appearance, and Actions
- Clothes, hair and eye color
- How the character moves

III. Thoughts and Feelings
- What the character says out loud
- What the character thinks or says to himself
- How he feels
- His moods

IV. Strengths and Weaknesses
- Fears, flaws, and quirks
- Special powers or skills

V. Personality Traits and Motives
- What kind of person is each character?
- What is it that each character most wants?
- What is it each character absolutely has to do?

CHARACTER DESCRIPTION RUBRIC

Goal/ Score	Writing Strategies and Applications	Writing Conventions
4	• Expository composition vividly describes each character's appearance, actions, thoughts, feelings, strengths, weaknesses, personality, and motives. • Each character's contribution to the plot or role in the story is fully described. • Character descriptions show not only revision but also incorporation of reader response comments. Manuscript has been thoroughly edited and revised to improve the meaning and focus of the writing.	• Writing contains few, if any, errors in grammar, punctuation, capitalization, spelling, and sentence structure. • The errors do not interfere with the reader's understanding of the writing.
3	• Expository composition clearly describes each character's appearance, actions, thoughts, feelings, strengths, weaknesses, personality, and motives. • Each character's contribution to the plot or role in the story is described. • Much or most of the editing and revising of the manuscript has been done to improve the meaning and focus of the writing.	• Writing contains some errors in grammar, punctuation, capitalization, spelling, and sentence structure. • The errors do not interfere with the reader's understanding of the writing.

CHARACTER DESCRIPTION RUBRIC
(Continued)

Goal/ Score	Writing Strategies and Applications	Writing Conventions
2	• Expository composition vaguely describes each character's appearance, actions, thoughts, feelings, strengths, weaknesses, personality, and motives. • Each character's contribution to the plot or role in the story may not be fully described. • Some editing and revising of the manuscript has been completed.	• Writing contains several errors in grammar, punctuation, capitalization, spelling, and sentence structure. • The errors may interfere with the reader's understanding of the writing.
1	• Expository composition fails to adequately describe each character's appearance, actions, thoughts, feelings, strengths, weaknesses, personality, and motives. • Each character's contribution to the plot or role in the story is not described. • Little or no editing or revising has been done to the manuscript to improve the meaning and focus of the writing.	• Writing contains numerous errors in grammar, punctuation, capitalization, spelling, and sentence structure. • The errors interfere with the reader's understanding of the writing.

Crafting the Characters

CHARACTER DESCRIPTION
READER RESPONSE

Readers should keep in mind that the response page should provide the writer with a balance of compliments that encourage and delicately worded suggestions for improvement. For the character description, readers should write comments that reflect on the following qualities:

- Has the author created six story characters (hero, helper, sidekick, two conflict characters, and a villain) that are lively and realistic?
- Has the author used a variety of precise, colorful adjectives and sensory details to describe the appearances, actions, thoughts, feelings, strengths, weaknesses, personality traits, and motives of each character?
- Has the author used a variety of topic sentences to introduce each new character trait?
- Has the author clearly identified the role or contribution that each character will have in the story?

Name of Reader 1: _____

Comments: _____

_____

_____

_____

_____

Name of Reader 2: _____

Comments: _____

_____

_____

_____

_____

CHARACTER DESCRIPTION
READER RESPONSE
(Continued)

Name of Reader 3: _____

Comments: _____

_____

_____

_____

_____

TYPES OF CHARACTERS

You'll need to have a few characters for your story. As we've already seen, stories of fantasy generally have three good guys and three bad guys. Here are the character types you will want to choose from: one hero or heroine (this is the protagonist or main character), one side-kick, one helper, a villain, and one or two conflict characters. Altogether then, your story, if you follow this basic formula, will have a total of six characters.

HERO/HEROINE/PROTAGONIST

This is the character we follow through the story. Heroes come in all sizes, shapes, and colors. Some heroes are small, fairly ordinary, and often innocent in the ways of the world. Others are big, extraordinary, and very knowledgeable about world affairs. However, more often than not, most heroes have a fairly typical back story. These are some of the common characteristics of the hero's past:

MYSTERIOUS OR UNUSUAL BIRTH
Heroes have often had some type of mysterious or unusual birth.

PROPHECY
Heroes have prophecies told about them; someone "in the know" predicts that something grand is supposed to happen to them. They've been told, "You will one day become a great hero." And the hero copes with the curse and blessing of having to live up to this prophecy. Sometimes the prophecy told is that their job is to overthrow the present order, or to restore a vanished order.

SECLUDED CHILDHOOD
Often, the hero was secluded during childhood. She has been kept secret or shielded from the ways of the world. Sometimes heroes have been living among humble people in a simple, pastoral setting.

UNUSUAL NATURE (HIDDEN GIFTS)
The hero often has an unusual nature or some sort of hidden gift or ability. This hidden gift sometimes makes the hero something of an outsider. Often, he is looked down upon or even feared because of his unusual nature.

ENDURING ORPHAN

Many heroes in stories of fantasy have somehow lost one or both of their parents. Being an orphan can help a reader feel sympathetic to the hero. And being an orphan gives the hero the opportunity to go out into the world alone. Parents are not around to limit the hero's explorations.

VILLAIN/VILLAINESS/ANTAGONIST/LURKING EVIL

This character works against the hero. Traditionally, the evil in fantasy is personified by someone of extraordinary and perverse power whose goal in life is to bring the greatest possible misery to the largest number of good honest folk. The problem with villains is that you can't make them totally despicable. They have to possess some quality that makes us interested in them. But you don't want to make them too interesting, because if you do, they could become more engaging than the good and dutiful hero. Weird sometimes works. Weird characters are always interesting. Villains have often had an improper upbringing and this twists their personality.

HELPER/MENTOR

This character is usually a positive figure who aids, guides, trains, or teaches the hero. The mentor supplies the hero with certain gifts, objects, or words of power. The helper often speaks with authority or is inspired by divine wisdom. Helpers represent the good within us, the aspect of our personality that is connected with all things. The helper is usually a wiser, nobler, more knowing character. Sometimes the helper is a former hero who has survived life's early trials and is now passing on the knowledge and wisdom gained. Other times, helpers are on a hero's journey of their own. We call this kind of helper a *fallen* helper. A fallen helper is someone who is experiencing a crisis, or perhaps dealing with problems of aging, or approaching the threshold of death. In any case, they have fallen from their heroic path. In this case, your story's hero needs the helper to pull himself together one more time, and there is serious doubt that he can do it.

SIDEKICK/BUDDY/CONFIDANT

The sidekick is usually the hero's friend, buddy, or confidant. The sidekick, besides sometimes helping the hero, usually allows the reader to observe another side of the hero. Information about the hero is more

Crafting the Characters

naturally revealed through the use of the sidekick. The sidekick prompts the hero to reveal deeply held information about his feelings, motivations, or history. The sidekick could be any number of personalities. Sometimes they are comical characters who, with all of their flaws or weaknesses, get the hero into or even out of a jam.

CONFLICT CHARACTERS AND CREATURES

Conflict characters usually provide some type of roadblock for the hero and sidekick. Typically, a fantasy creature portrays the role of the conflict character. Of course, you'll want to consult the description of fantasy characters and creatures provided in the next section.

FANTASY CHARACTERS

DWARFS

Dwarfs are a race of small men and women who usually live underground. They are expert miners and metalworkers. They also have magical powers that enable them to find the precious metals that they work into every kind of weapon or artifact imaginable. They are especially good at making swords and armor. Dwarfs have short, stocky bodies; enormous heads; weathered faces; and long, sometimes braided beards. They are usually seen wearing long, hooded cloaks and armor. They also regularly carry a big, heavy club and heavy shield.

ELVES

Elves are a race of characters who usually live in the forest. They look a lot like humans but are much more handsome and beautiful. They have long hair and pointed ears. Elves have a great deal of practical wisdom, and they have the ability to see into the future. Elves love to party and enjoy dancing and singing joyfully all night long until they disappear, leaving nothing behind except footprints in the wet grass.

Crafting the Characters

FAIRIES

Fairies look like miniature humans with gossamer wings. They are about six to twelve inches tall. Fairies are typically very difficult to find, for they are extremely proficient at hiding themselves. Sometimes fairies can be seen during special times of the year; certain seasons or particular phases of the moon are good for spotting fairies. Fairies are frequently looked upon as fragile, carefree creatures, but in fact the males are heroic fighters who protect their homes against invasion by gremlins, goblins, and other nasty creatures. Fairies are usually mischievous toward humans, but sometimes they have a sincere yearning to assist and delight.

GIANTS

Giants are huge men and women who are neither mortal nor immortal. Sometimes they possess magical powers, but often they are just huge, clumsy characters who settle in various parts of the earth, such as mountain ranges and forests. Giants typically cause great mischief by joining in human quarrels, gobbling up flocks of sheep, drinking rivers dry, trampling crops underfoot, or ripping mountains apart. They are especially good at throwing huge boulders.

Crafting the Characters

GOBLINS

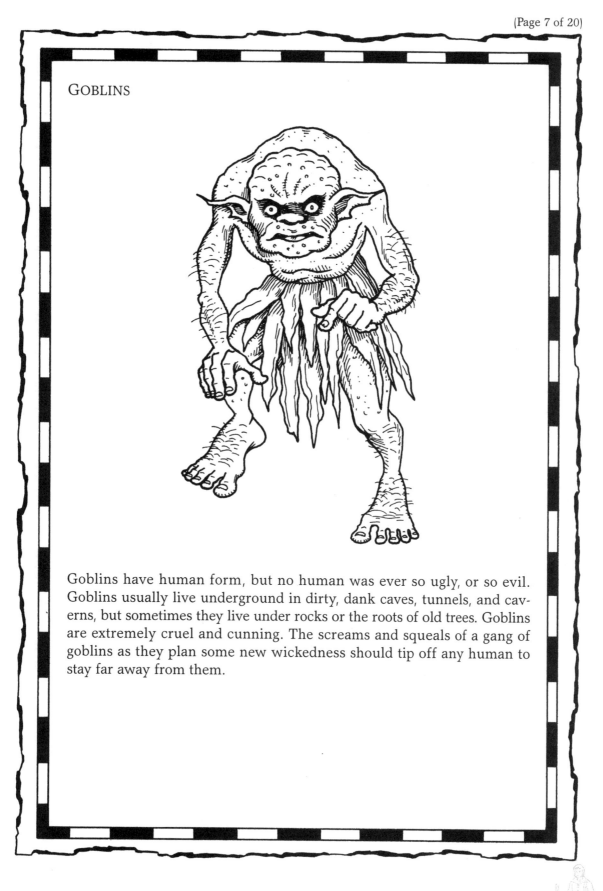

Goblins have human form, but no human was ever so ugly, or so evil. Goblins usually live underground in dirty, dank caves, tunnels, and caverns, but sometimes they live under rocks or the roots of old trees. Goblins are extremely cruel and cunning. The screams and squeals of a gang of goblins as they plan some new wickedness should tip off any human to stay far away from them.

GNOMES

Gnomes are about six inches tall and have an endless supply of good humor. Typically, gnomes are helpful and harmless. They also have a keen insight into the character of all living and nonliving creatures and objects. This enables them to easily influence and cooperate with trees, animals, plants, and every other creation. Gnomes live in colonies underground and are particularly good at moving through the earth. They can often be found in human gardens, seemingly helping to take care of the many plants and vegetables thriving there.

GREMLINS

Crafting the Characters

Gremlins are small, green, mischievous characters who usually live near or inside various tools or machines. Gremlins use their advanced knowledge of tools and machines to make life difficult for people. This so-called gremlin effect often appears when a hammer hits a thumb, a screwdriver slips, the paint runs, the toast burns, a clock or watch stops, or a car breaks down.

LEPRECHAUNS

Leprechauns are fairy cobblers who make shoes for other fairies. They usually hibernate underground during the winter and come out in the summer. Leprechauns are happy little fellows dressed in green, with a red cap, leather apron, and buckled shoes. Leprechauns often know where to find hidden treasure and are excitedly desired for that exact reason.

ORCS

Orcs are an advanced, and dangerous, type of goblin. Some say that they were once elves who have been tortured, enslaved, and mutilated. Orcs are large, strong, and muscular. They have sharp, pointed teeth; wide faces; and slanting eyes. Orcs typically live underground and regularly battle dwarfs and goblins for caves.

Crafting the Characters

MERFOLK

Mermaids and mermen live beneath the ocean. Merfolk are human in appearance above the waist, but below they have large, whale-like tails. They are capable of changing their tails into legs, so that they may occasionally walk on land. Merfolk usually live close to the coast where the water is shallow. Most mermaids possess incredible beauty. Mermen are sturdy, strong, and muscular. Merfolk and humans are extremely attracted to one another. But because relations between the two are so complex, the end result is usually tragic.

TROLLS

Trolls are extremely dumb, grotesque giants who live in forests and mountains. Some trolls never venture out from their deep underground caverns. But, if they do, they only come out at night. Many trolls have been known to turn to stone if the light of the sun ever hits them. Trolls are usually very aggressive toward humans and will even eat them if they are hungry and no other food is available. Trolls are also known to peek through windows and may even reach through an open one to fondle a variety of human belongings.

Crafting the Characters

WIZARDS

Wizards are usually wise old men with long, gray beards; pointed hats; long cloaks; big, black boots; and sturdy staffs. Wizards have learned their crafts of wizardry through an extended apprenticeship of study and research. Wizards are often very friendly with fairies, elves, and other creatures and animals. A wizard's power depends on the extent of his learning and experience. Therefore, the oldest wizards usually have the greatest magical powers. Wizards are also capable of deciphering ancient texts and tomes that contain many little-known spells and magical incantations.

FANTASY CREATURES

DRAGONS

Dragons are the nastiest of creatures. They're in the reptile kingdom, and therefore classified as serpents. Dragons typically have unusually sharp vision and are also known to be quite sly, clever, and wise. Most dragons can fly and have the ability to breathe fire. Dragons are often guardians or sentinels of all kinds of treasures. Like other reptiles, dragons usually stay close to their own territory; they hardly ever eat and are satisfied with the occasional cow, goat, or human. For these reasons, a dragon that is guarding a treasure is nearly always at its post, either resting at the entry to the hoard or soaring above it to keep a lookout for possible intruders.

LEVIATHANS

A leviathan is an enormous fire-breathing sea monster. It is said that the water boils when a leviathan swims on the surface of the sea. Leviathans are known to breathe smoke from their nostrils and flame from their mouths. Their skin is extremely tough and covered with scales as big as shields on their back and belly. Harpoons, javelins, and spears simply bounce off a leviathan's armored hide. Leviathans are ruthless and fearless. They also have hearts as hard and cold as stone; they simply are completely untroubled by any efforts to catch them. The sight of this scary sea creature, with its fiery eyes cutting through the waves of the sea, will put terror in the heart of any pursuer.

PHOENIXES

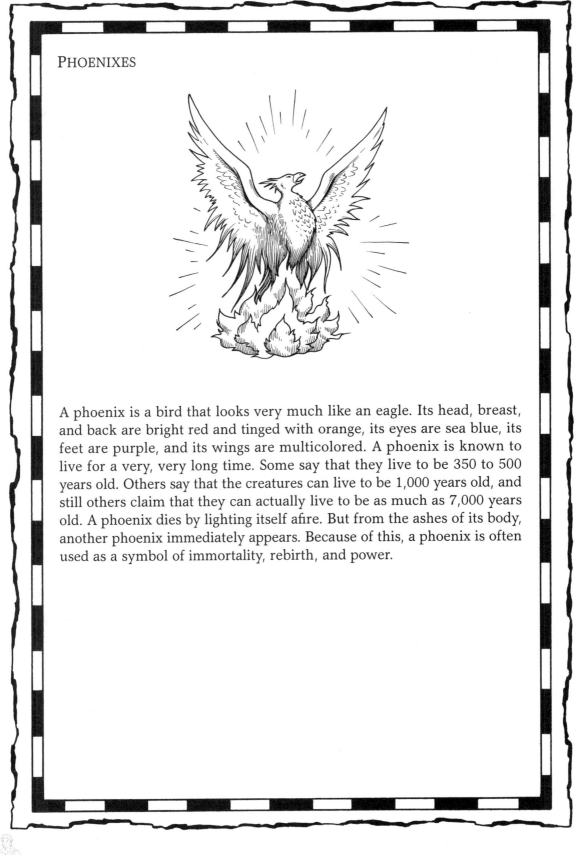

A phoenix is a bird that looks very much like an eagle. Its head, breast, and back are bright red and tinged with orange, its eyes are sea blue, its feet are purple, and its wings are multicolored. A phoenix is known to live for a very, very long time. Some say that they live to be 350 to 500 years old. Others say that the creatures can live to be 1,000 years old, and still others claim that they can actually live to be as much as 7,000 years old. A phoenix dies by lighting itself afire. But from the ashes of its body, another phoenix immediately appears. Because of this, a phoenix is often used as a symbol of immortality, rebirth, and power.

UNICORNS

Unicorns are white horses with long flowing tails and manes. The most interesting characteristic of a unicorn is its long, sharp, spiraled horn that grows right out of the middle of its forehead. This horn can be used as a dangerous weapon, capable of piercing almost anything, or it can be used for its magical power to detect and negate almost any poison. It is for these reasons that unicorn horns are much desired by humans. Most unicorns are known to be the swiftest animals roving the plains or rambling through the forest. Unicorns are usually solitary creatures that do not pasture in herds. Unicorns have one weakness, however: they can be trapped by a young maiden in the woods. Affectionate unicorns really like young, gentle maidens, and they will approach them and lay their handsome heads gently in a maiden's lap. Only then will the unicorn become easy prey for the hunters seeking the power of their magical horns.

TALKING TREES

Often found in stories of fantasy are talking trees. Sometimes these trees talk to characters in need of assistance, but sometimes they can also cast a dangerous spell. Talking to trees is rather difficult, however. Most find it hard to hear and understand the sound of their strange voices. Some say they sound like a combination of sighing, murmuring, and groaning. Larger trees have deep thick voices, whereas smaller and slimmer trees whisper so quietly as to be almost inaudible.

MINOTAURS, CENTAURS, AND SPHINXES

Minotaurs are creatures that are half man and half bull. They usually have a human body with a bull's head. Centaurs are creatures that are half horse and half man. They are human from the waist up and a horse from the waist down. A sphinx is a winged creature with a lion's body and a woman's head. All of these creatures were created in ancient mythology. They could find a place in your fantasy story. Or, you might want to invent a creature of your own. How many animals put together will create your fantasy creature?

Crafting the Characters

CHARACTER ILLUSTRATION

Character type (hero/heroine, sidekick, helper, villain or conflict character/creature): _____

Character name: _____

Provide a brief written description of this character:

_____

_____

_____

_____

_____

NAMING YOUR CHARACTERS

You've got to name your characters, don't you? Well, now's the time to start.

Sometimes, your characters' names can say an awful lot about who they are.

For example: How about ... Humon Gusliar? Well, you know he's got to be a *humongous liar*. And then there's ... Ob Noxious. No need to tell you what kind of person she is!

You could try creating a name that sounds like an action or movement the character repeats often. For example, say a villain hacks away at everything in his path. He's always destroying something. He's a hacker. You could name him ... Hacker or Harak, for example.

Your turn. Start playing with some names. Don't worry if the names start sounding like nonsense. Nonsense names can come in handy when crafting your characters.

Hero name options:

Villain name options:

Sidekick name options:

Helper name options:

Conflict characters name options:

CHARACTER QUALITIES

Characters have a huge importance on your story's plot and theme. So it's important to be able to thoroughly describe each of your characters. You'll need to use plenty of concrete sensory details as well. Here are the categories you'll need to describe:

CONTRIBUTION TO THE PLOT

First of all, you'll need to tell us what role each character is going to play: hero, villain, sidekick, helper, villain's sidekick, or conflict character. Each of these character types will contribute to the plot in a unique and essential way.

LOOKS AND APPEARANCE

Readers need to know how each character looks. How do they appear to the reader? Are they messy or neat? What sort of clothes do they wear? What does their face look like? What kind of body do they have? What color is their hair? How long is it? What color eyes do they have? How people look can tell a great deal about their character.

ACTIONS

Next, we need to know how each character moves. What kind of gestures, quirks, habits, or idiosyncrasies do they regularly exhibit? Do they walk with a limp? Do they plod along slowly? Do they skip along happily with a spring in their step? Do they have a weird sort of twitch? We also need to know what kind of words or speech patterns they regularly show. Do they slur their words? Talk rapidly? What kinds of things do they regularly say? All these things can tell the reader a lot about each character.

THOUGHTS

Everybody talks to themselves, right? We call this *interior monologue*. This *talking in your head* is a way to show us much about a character. Is the character an optimist, always upbeat and happy? Or a pessimist, always downbeat and defeatist?

FEELINGS

Another thing we need to know about all the characters is their feelings. This is where you can tell us all about your characters' moods. What do they regularly feel? Are they always angry? Sad? Happy? Or are they really complex and have a tendency to show a complicated combination of feelings? What do they fear? What do they believe in? What is it that they value most?

STRENGTHS AND WEAKNESSES

All characters must have a few strengths and weaknesses. Having both strengths and weaknesses, even if that character is the hero or villain, will help make him more interesting and multidimensional. Nobody likes a perfect person. Perfect people don't seem real. Remember, a hero or heroine's imperfections are what make him or her likeable and real. All characters, no matter who they are, have some weakness. It could be a specific character flaw—such as personality—or simple mess-ups that they create. On the other hand, if you're writing fantasy, it's more than likely that sooner or later, your characters are going to work some magic. Do your characters have any magical powers? What special strengths do your characters have?

PERSONALITY TRAITS

When someone asks, "Yeah, but what kind of person is she?" what they're really asking about is that person's personality. Personality is the sum total of a person's attitudes, interests, behaviors, emotions, roles, and other individual traits that last for long periods of time. Personality is what makes each of your characters unusual and distinctive. Create a character personality trait profile unique to each individual.

MOTIVES

All of your characters want something. And they will do nearly anything to get it. So start thinking. What are your characters' deepest desires? What do they want to gain, protect, win, or discover? Or is there something that they desperately must get away from? Readers need to understand why characters want what they want. Your characters will act more intensely, more courageously, more foolishly, and in far more interesting ways if they are following their deepest desires. So, you must identify each character's motives.

Most important of all is that the main character definitely have a motive. A motivated hero creates action, gets other people moving and reacting. And that's the key to the plot, which draws us through your story. Finding your hero's deepest desire will move your story along. The more intense your hero's desire, the less effort you'll need to put in to move your story along.

Your hero may make a few wrong turns, or go through a dangerous door, or bump into all kinds of interesting things, but he must be in relentless pursuit of something. Remember, if your story is to be worth reading, this must be the most critical moment in your hero's life. So what is it that he absolutely must have?

Keep in mind, too, that your story's theme should reflect upon your main character's desires, purpose, vision, or mission. The theme helps explain why your main character has the motivation to do what it is she must do.

Still having a difficult time deciding on your hero's deepest desires? Well, here are a few possibilities you might want to consider:

The need to get or acquire something:

- To obtain a special elixir to save someone's life
- To help someone recover jewels or gold
- To win a wife or husband
- To return to a place visited in a dream
- To save the world, human race, a species of animal, a forest
- To find a home or to get a home back
- To return to parents, grandparents, or sibling
- To get back parents, grandparents, or sibling

The need to avoid or escape something:
Perhaps your story is moved along by the hero's need to avoid some stinky, gooey, icky, nasty, mean thing growing behind him.

The need to both escape and to get:
Here you have the worst of situations. Something is coming up behind the heroine while she is also in pursuit of something else.

It is extremely important to make sure that you know your main character's motives, because later on, when working on your story's plot line, these motives are going to help set your hero's mission in motion. It will set him on the path, the journey, which will get your story going.

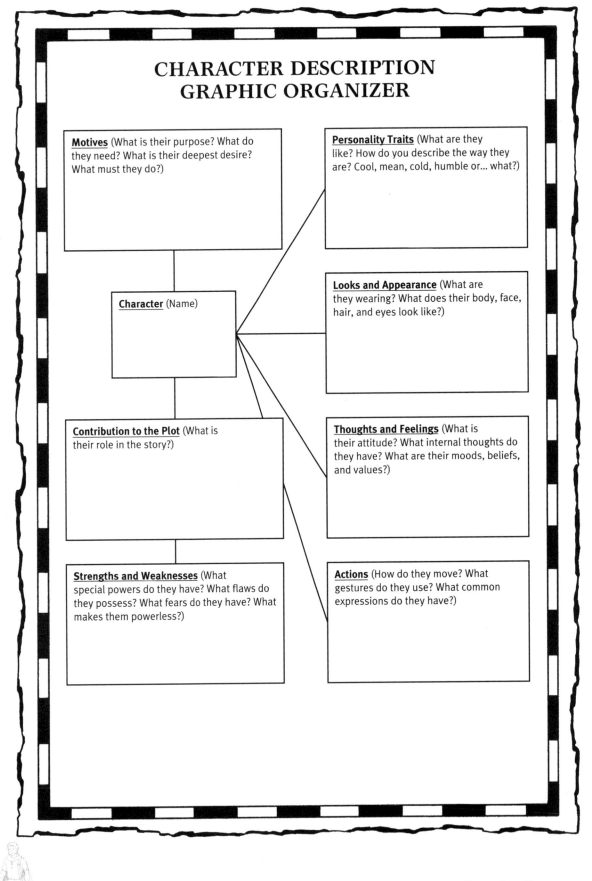

CHARACTER DESCRIPTION
GRAPHIC ORGANIZER

Motives (What is their purpose? What do they need? What is their deepest desire? What must they do?)

Personality Traits (What are they like? How do you describe the way they are? Cool, mean, cold, humble or… what?)

Character (Name)

Looks and Appearance (What are they wearing? What does their body, face, hair, and eyes look like?)

Contribution to the Plot (What is their role in the story?)

Thoughts and Feelings (What is their attitude? What internal thoughts do they have? What are their moods, beliefs, and values?)

Strengths and Weaknesses (What special powers do they have? What flaws do they possess? What fears do they have? What makes them powerless?)

Actions (How do they move? What gestures do they use? What common expressions do they have?)

Crafting the Characters

PERSONALITY TRAITS

Having trouble deciding what personality traits your characters will have? Take a look at the words in this list. While looking, keep a specific character type (hero, helper, sidekick, conflict character, villain) in mind. When you find a character trait that you think fits, write the word (or words) in the appropriate character space on the next sheet.

mean	generous	stubborn
leader	fighter	neat
independent	fun-loving	timid
rude	unselfish	resourceful
conceited	selfish	messy
creative	witty	hard-working
stingy	curious	sad
nasty	lazy	wild
humble	carefree	adventurous
calm	quiet	crazy
happy	busy	proud
imaginative	caring	friendly
thoughtful	ambitious	funny
dreamer	dainty	loving
considerate	silly	mischievous
cheerful	lovable	serious
helpful	daring	gentle
respectful	gullible	honest
energetic	cooperative	courageous
responsible	bold	bossy
self-confident	loyal	intelligent
determined	joyful	brave
successful	shy	demanding

PERSONALITY TRAITS
(Continued)

Hero: _____

_____

_____

Sidekick: _____

_____

_____

Helper: _____

_____

_____

Conflict Character #1: _____

_____

_____

Conflict Character #2: _____

_____

_____

Villain: _____

_____

_____

Crafting the Characters

CHARACTER ACTIONS:
HOW DO THEY MOVE?

Having trouble deciding how your characters will move? You might want to take a look at this list of words. While looking, keep a specific character in mind. When you find a character movement, action, or stance that you think fits, write the word (or words) in the appropriate space on the next sheet.

amble	prance	swagger
bounce	prowl	tiptoe
slither	ramble	totter
clump	jog	trample
stomp	sashay	tromp
flutter	loaf	trudge
gallop	saunter	waddle
glide	scamper	creep
hobble	chug	whisk
stroll	scuffle	wobble
hop	meander	zip
run	shamble	spring
jounce	slide	flit
leap	slither	strut
lope	slosh	stumble
lumber	zoom	mosey
march	sprint	patter
patter	stagger	frolic
rumble	flash	slouch
squirm	plod	lurk
fidget	sneak	hunch
bobble	dillydally	wiggle

CHARACTER ACTIONS:
HOW DO THEY MOVE?
(Continued)

Hero: _____

_____

_____

Sidekick: _____

_____

_____

Helper: _____

_____

_____

Conflict Character #1: _____

_____

_____

Conflict Character #2: _____

_____

_____

Villain: _____

_____

_____

CHARACTER HISTORY

Every character has a history. They have all lived a full life, even before your story started. The more you know about a character's history, the more real and lifelike he or she will seem. All of these facts about each character's history might not find their way into your story, but these important details will help you to decide how each of your characters will behave once your story gets started. So spend a little time working out your character's history.

Name of character: _____

Role in your story (circle one): hero/heroine, sidekick, helper, villain, or conflict character/creature

Where was this character born? _____

Was this character rich, poor, or in between? _____

What life experiences—good or bad—does this character remember most?
_____

Who was the most influential person (positive or negative) in this character's life? _____
_____
_____

Who raised this character? His or her parents, or someone else?
_____
_____

Did these people argue and fight, or were they happy all the time?
_____
_____

How did this character feel about the people who raised him or her?
_____
_____

Was this character's family nurturing or rough?
_____
_____

CHARACTER HISTORY
(Continued)

What kind of trouble upset the family? What emotions couldn't be expressed?

_____

_____

Was this character an obedient child or a difficult one?

_____

_____

Did this character move a lot or stay put in one house?

_____

_____

Did this character have brothers or sisters, or was this character an only child?

_____

_____

Did this character have many friends, real or imaginary?

_____

_____

Did the character spend a lot of time alone?

_____

_____

In a group of friends, was this character a leader or a follower?

_____

_____

Did the character "fit in"? Or, did he do things he should not have, or pretend to be someone or something he wasn't, so that he *could* fit in?

_____

_____

CHARACTER VOICES

What does the reader hear your characters saying? And how, exactly, will your characters talk? Will they whine and complain? Be mean or nasty? Or will they be cheerful or goofy? Will they talk rapidly or will the pace of their words plod along? Will they speak with a stutter or lisp? Or will they speak clearly and properly?

More than likely, each of your characters will be doing some talking. Some of what they say will be said out loud. Other times, they will talk internally to themselves. The things your characters say, and how they say them, will reveal much about their personalities. No two characters should use the same words or talk in the same style. Ideally, you want each of your characters to have a strong voice. And you definitely don't want them to sound just like you! You'll want the characters you create to sound real! So give them their own voices.

Let's hear from your characters. What are they going to be saying throughout your story? And perhaps more important, how will they say it? Give your characters their own distinctive voices.

HERO'S HANKERINGS

To hanker is to want something very badly and persistently. What is it that your hero hankers over? Is your hero a happy hankerer? "Let's go! We need to save the day!" Or is she a hapless hankerer (someone who really would rather stay at home)? "Oh man! Why do I have to do this? I only wanted a peaceful life!"

HEARING FROM THE HEART OF THE HELPER

What is it that the helper tells the hero? What heartfelt remarks does the helper have? "Oh, little one. I am only here to help you! Be not afraid."

SIDEKICK'S WISECRACKS

Sidekicks are often humorous characters. Sometimes a wisecrack can come from a sidekick. What is it that your sidekick will say? And more important, how will the sidekick say it?

THE VILLAIN'S VENOMOUS VITRIOL

Vitriol is extreme bitterness and hatred toward somebody or something. But *venomous* vitriol is even worse. And if the venomous vitriol comes from the villain … *v*atch out! "I am the master of the universe. I alone shall rule the world!" *V*at *v*ill *v*e hear from *your* villain?

Crafting the Characters

THEME THREAD: CONTRASTING CHARACTERS

To help thread your story's theme it is useful to contrast the hero with the villain. When these two characters have contrasting personalities, all sorts of conflicts and clashes can result. Contrasts between these two characters can add fuel and tension to your story and make the plot more dynamic. Explore the differences between these two characters. Plus, see if you can find a way for this contrast to help thread your story's theme. In other words, how can the contrast between your hero and villain reflect upon what *you* want to say?

Contrasting Characters Table

Hero:	Villain:
Actions:	Actions:
Motives:	Motives:
Appearance:	Appearance:
Thoughts and feelings:	Thoughts and feelings:
Personality traits:	Personality traits:

Describe how the differences between your hero and your villain can add fuel and tension to the plot of your story.

_____

_____

_____

_____

_____

_____

When your hero and villain meet, what kind of conflict could arise because of these differences?

_____

_____

_____

_____

_____

What might your hero tell your villain when they finally meet? Is there anything in what the hero has to say that could reflect upon what *you* want to say?

_____

_____

_____

_____

_____

_____

_____

Crafting the Characters

Chapter Six

Plotting the Path

The hero must venture forth from the world of commonsense consciousness into a region of super-natural wonder. There he encounters fabulous forces—demons and angels, dragons and helping spirits. After a fierce battle, he wins a decisive victory over the powers of darkness. Then he returns from his mysterious adventure with the gift of knowledge or fire, which he bestows on his fellow man.

—Joseph Campbell

Now that your heroic student writers have contemplated a theme to thread, formed their fantasylands, set their stories' surroundings, and crafted their characters, it's time for them to plot their protagonists' path. An easy way for students to create a plot is to help them think of it as a perilous journey that their story's hero must take across their newly created fantasyland.

Yes, a story's plot line is an outward path full of adventure, conflicts, trials, and tribulations, but it is also an inward path of the hero's quest for identity. Therefore, when plotting the path of the protagonist, students should also try to display their characters' personalities. They should show us how and what their characters are learning. And the path plotted should provide many interesting opportunities for the crafted cast of characters and creatures to be brave, cowardly, smart, foolish, good, or evil.

For this part of the story creation process, two basic paths are available for the plotting. The first is the *linear path*, for which a prompt, rubric, and reader response page are provided. The second, the *circular path*, is offered as an alternative to give students a more in-depth understanding of the hero's journey. You may want to have students start first with the linear path, and when completed, distribute the materials for the circular path so that they may travel further into the "deeper" aspects.

Once students are aware of the basic plot line structures, allow them the opportunity to negotiate a change if desired. Students may want to add a conflict or two, or twist the plot in a way that makes sense. As long as they can diagram the changes, and explain the trajectory of the path and the content of the scenes, any change they wish to make, if enthusiastically presented, should be allowed.

And so, with the plotting of the protagonist's path complete, and with a full arsenal of writing skills in their possession, our student heroes will be prepared to depart on their journey into the story-writing world. They will have appeased the guardians of the threshold and be given access to the kingdom of narrative.

James Henry Trotter's Trip Across the Atlantic, in *James and the Giant Peach*, by Roald Dahl

The path that James, his troupe of insects, and the peach travel from the hills of England, across the Atlantic, and all the way to the pinnacle of the Empire State Building in New York City provides a wonderful opportunity for exploring text structure and organization. A side view of Trotter's trip reveals a clear linear plot line structure.

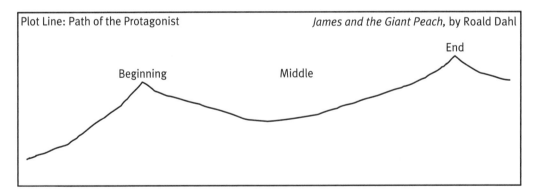

We created this side view of the protagonist's path in the classroom while analyzing Roald Dahl's terrific work. First, I gave the students a copy of the preceding drawing. Then, students went to work filling in the spaces, drawing, coloring, and describing the various steps (exposition, complication, conflicts, climax, and resolution) of the story's plot line.

As you can see from Justin's drawing, the story's beginning—exposition and complication—is depicted by James's parents and a rhinoceros, and then, by Aunt Sponge and Spiker's queer ramshackle house, peach and tree, and James, on a high hill in the south of England. The middle is the series of conflicts encountered as the peach and passengers travel across the Atlantic Ocean. The exciting

Justin Chow's depiction of Trotter's trip
across the Atlantic.

climax is drawn as a giant peach spiked upon the pinnacle of the Empire State Building. Finally, the story resolves with James living happily ever after in the giant stone of the peach nestled comfortably in New York's Central Park.

Justin was also asked to describe each step along the way. For each conflict, Justin wrote not only on the nature of the conflict but also on how it was resolved. His drawing and descriptions caught my eye—hence, my sharing his work with you now.

Analyzing a story's plot line in such a way helps students understand a basic story structure that they may not have known existed. This process alone helps students feel more comfortable, because they now are aware of the foundation from which to build a whole, cohesive story.

If you are interested in analyzing a story's plot line this way, you will first need to pass out the Rubric for Narrative Plot Line, the first worksheet in the student activity pages of this chapter. As always, it is helpful to review with your students the rubric that will evaluate their plot lines so that they become aware of the specific criteria or objectives they must address. Before beginning, read the rubric in class, discuss its contents, have students highlight or circle key phrases, and challenge them to set a goal or score they would like to achieve. Make sure to remind them that they must not only identify each conflict in the story you are analyzing but also identify how each conflict is resolved.

Taylor Thomas's Trip Around the Fertile Crescent, in *The Rock of Jerusalem*, by Mr. Gust

To impress on my students the fact that "real" writers actually do the very thing that I was asking them all to do, I decided to bring in the plot line for the story that I was working on at the time. Since I had spent so much time trying to work out how this story might proceed, I decided to think of myself as one of the "real" writers to whom I was referring.

When I unveiled the plot line, which I had drawn on a long, long piece of butcher paper, the first thing I heard was, "You're not done!" "Yeah," said another child. "You've got at least four scenes to describe. See," he said, standing up and pointing, "there's four blank boxes in your plot line." I had to defend myself: "But … there must be at least a dozen other scenes that have been fully described. And look, there are three separate plot lines that all have to interweave as the story progresses. This is a complicated story! Give me a break." Most of the class agreed to let me off the hook for now, but only on the condition that I fully explain the plot line. I grinned, and promptly jumped into my presentation, modeling all the skills I was hoping they would demonstrate in their own plot line presentations.

Mr. Gust presents the plot line of the second book in
The Taylor Thomas Trilogy: The Rock of Jerusalem.

Plot Line Assignment

For this assignment students will be asked to create a detailed description of their story's plot line. To guide them through this process, first pass out the plot line prompt, rubric, and listener response (for this assignment, students will be asked to *orally* describe the events of the story) pages. This will give students a clear vision of the final product and help them understand what is required of them. Once everyone is headed in the right direction,

Adventures in Fantasy

guide your students through the linear path activity to help them understand the various steps along the protagonist's path. Finally, pass out the Linear Plot Line Graphic Organizer and let your students go to work designing their story's plot line. When everyone is finished, have students get together during a writers' workshop with their Plot Line Listener Response pages so that they can orally describe how their stories will proceed. You may also want to implement the Mission in Motion: The Complication activity to highlight the importance of identifying a strong enough reason for the hero to set off on his long and arduous journey.

Plot Line Prompt

To get your students started on their story's plot line, first pass out the prompt and read it over with your class. You will notice that this prompt presents students with a new challenge: This time, students will be required to give an oral presentation of their story's plot line.

Plot Line Rubric

The plot line rubric will be used to guide students to verbally describe their plots. Using the Linear Plot Line Graphic Organizer, their maps, and their character illustrations as guides, students will be required to describe the following:

- The complication, and why the hero's mission has been set in motion
- Where each event or scene will take place on their map
- How each conflict will be resolved
- How the complication will be resolved during the climax
- When and where each character will be introduced in the story
- How the story will exhibit a rise in tension and action as it progresses to the climax

Plot Line Listener Response

After students have completed their plot lines, they will need to take it, the rubric, and the listener response page, along with their maps and character illustrations (if necessary), and get together with a few partners to orally describe the plot of their story. Students really appreciate the opportunity to get together with classmates and point to their maps while describing all the exciting events and strange characters that their heroes will encounter in their stories.

The Linear Path

As already noted, the hero's journey is often thought of as a linear path. This activity takes students through the steps and phases of a story: from the beginning, through the middle, into an ending. This minilesson describes how to write an exposition, complication, two conflicts, a climax, and a resolution. After taking a quick look at the student pages provided, you can either provide a quick lecture with notes and illustrations drawn on the board, or have students read the pages through any method imaginable (whole class, in groups or pairs, individually).

Linear Plot Line Graphic Organizer

All students have to do is sketch out an idea to show what will happen in each of the six scenes. They should briefly describe who will be in each scene, where it will take place, and how the conflicts will be resolved.

Mission in Motion: The Complication

When students begin to construct their plot lines, it is imperative for them to make a strong connection with the complication of the story. We don't want students to miss creating a good enough reason for the hero or heroine to go on this arduous journey. Student writers must provide the reader with a good enough reason to continue reading. Students need to know, and remember, that the complication is what must be solved by the story's end. Students must make the complication *complicated* enough to keep the reader's interest peaked until the exciting climax, when the complication is finally resolved.

The Circular Path

Much has been written about the hero's path. Joseph Campbell in his seminal book *The Hero with a Thousand Faces* introduced a circular plot line as a common story structure involving heroic adventures. In this circular path, there are a total of eight basic steps to take. Pass out the reproducible student pages, read over the eight steps of the journey, and then invite your students to plot the circular path their story's hero or heroine will take. Students can then use this plot line, and the eight scenes that go with it, to either guide the writing of their stories or simply to gain a deeper understanding of the basic structure of their hero's journey.

Theme Thread: Traveling Inward

To continue the effort of threading a theme through their stories, try having students reconnect with their hero. Invite students to explore what their heroes will learn as they progress along their journeys' path. This minilesson will also help students search inside themselves, to look for clues as to what their hero could learn. As writers look inside themselves, they should remember why they got started writing in the first place; that is, they should have a theme in mind. Remember, the theme is often an elusive element for young writers, so they will need all the help they can get to find a theme.

Theme Thread: The Resolution

For your students to succeed in the difficult task of threading a theme, it will be helpful for them to know exactly *how* their story will end. For this, they must

Adventures in Fantasy

focus on the resolution. When your students know how their story's complication will be resolved, they will know its theme, moral, point, or larger message.

Remember, each student's ending will express some part of his or her own particular vision of the world. Therefore, it is important that all their stories emanate from their own truths. Plus, knowing how their story will end will also help them know exactly where it must begin. That is because the ending they choose will tell them what is important to be told in the rest of their story. It will let them know what they want the reader to pay attention to right from the start.

Pass out the student reproducible worksheet provided, read it over with your class, and help your students become aware of a few alternative endings they may not have considered. For example, rather than the hero simply defeating the villain, they might want to consider having their heroes or heroines change something inside of themselves instead. Maybe the hero or heroine will make a new connection with the helper, or a sidekick, or even the villain himself. Or maybe the hero will turn away from someone in the story, like an immature and irresponsible friend who got him into the predicament to begin with. And if the villain is defeated and the circumstances surrounding the hero's life are changed, maybe it will only be the result of the hero killing the villain with kindness. Help your students see the alternatives.

Lupe Fuimaono and Dianne Quiday are busy at work comparing each other's plot lines and maps.

Using his new map, Christian Millan enthusiastically explains his plot line to John Rivera, Mark Flores, Chijioke Orjiakor, and Michael Songloke.

Thomas Jeffrey shares his story plot line and map with Francis De Guzman.

Adventures in Fantasy

Nicole Jeter, Ellen Kim, and Cheyenne Young spread out on the floor to describe their plot lines and maps.

Noel Parisi points out the location of a conflict on her fantasyland map.

RUBRIC FOR NARRATIVE PLOT LINE

Goal/Score	Writing Strategies and Applications
4	• Written response demonstrates well-developed reading comprehension skills and the ability to describe the exposition, complication, conflicts, climax, and resolution of a story. • Statements that identify and summarize the main conflicts of the plot and explain how they are resolved are well supported by detailed evidence of specific events from the story. • Response demonstrates a thorough understanding of a literary work. • Interpretations of text exhibit thoughtful reading.
3	• Written response demonstrates solid reading comprehension skills and the ability to describe the exposition, complication, conflicts, climax, and resolution of a story. • Statements that identify and summarize the main problems or conflicts of the plot and explain how they are resolved are supported by detailed evidence of specific events from the story. • Response demonstrates an adequate understanding of a literary work. • Interpretations exhibit careful reading.
2	• Written response demonstrates some reading comprehension skills and the ability to summarize and describe the exposition, complication, conflicts, climax, and resolution of a story. • Statements that identify and summarize the main problems or conflicts of the plot and explain how they are resolved are reported but lack detailed evidence of specific events from the story. • Response demonstrates a weak understanding of a literary work. • Interpretations exhibit slipshod, slapdash reading.
1	• Written response demonstrates little or no reading comprehension skills and the ability to describe the exposition, complication, conflicts, climax, and resolution of a story. • Statements that identify and summarize the main problems or conflicts of the plot and explain how they are resolved are not fully reported and lack any evidence of specific events from the story. • Response demonstrates a lack of understanding of a literary work. • Interpretations exhibit careless, thoughtless reading and understanding.

PLOT LINE PROMPT

Now that you have set your surroundings and crafted your characters, it's time to plot your protagonist's path. For your story, your hero or heroine will need to complete a journey across your fantasyland with all of its mysterious places and crazy characters. It's an outward path full of adventure, conflicts, trials, and tribulations, yet it's also an inward path of the protagonist's quest for growth and understanding.

Your plot, therefore, with all of its strange creatures and landscapes to bump into, should also dramatize your characters' personalities. Think of how and what your characters are learning as the story progresses. Your plot should also provide opportunities for your characters to be brave, cowardly, smart, foolish, good, and evil.

For each scene on the path you plot, you will want to use short phrases to describe the conflicts and how they are resolved. You will also want to use key names to identify the settings. And you must remember to list the characters involved.

Once you have completed the graphic organizer, you will be asked to describe, in detail, the specifics of your plot to potential readers of your story. For this exercise you must tell your story orally, out loud. But don't worry; you'll be able to use your map, character illustrations, the plot line graphic organizer, and rubric to guide you along the way.

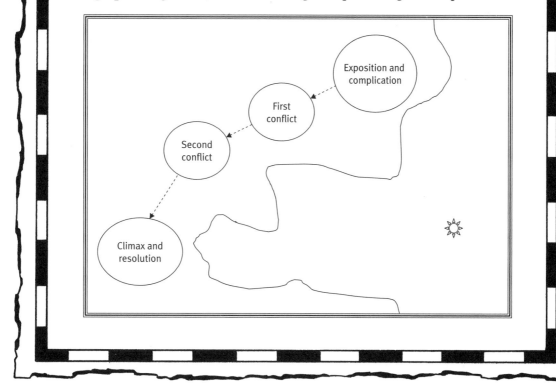

PLOT LINE RUBRIC

Goal/Score	Writing Strategies and Applications
4	• The author has a complete understanding of what will happen in each scene. • The complication is fully identified and the author clearly understands why the hero's mission has been set in motion. • The author can specifically identify where each event will take place on his or her map. • The author can clearly describe how each conflict will be resolved. • The author can thoroughly explain how the complication will be resolved in the climax. • The author is certain about when and where each character will be introduced in the story. • There is an obvious rise in tension and action as the story progresses to the climax.
3	• The author understands what will happen in each scene. • The complication is identified and the author understands why the hero's mission has been set in motion. • The author can identify where each event will take place on his or her map. • The author can describe how each conflict will be resolved. • The author can explain how the complication will be resolved in the climax. • The author knows when and where each character will be introduced in the story. • There is a rise in tension and action as the story progresses to the climax.

PLOT LINE RUBRIC
(Continued)

Goal/Score	Writing Strategies and Applications
2	• The author has some understanding of what will happen in each scene. • The complication is identified but the author may not clearly understand why the hero's mission has been set in motion. • The author is not clear on where each event will take place on his or her map. • The author may not be able to identify how each conflict will be resolved. • The author is unclear about how the complication will be resolved in the climax. • The author is uncertain when and where each character will be introduced in the story. • The rise in tension and action as the story progresses to the climax is not clearly apparent.
1	• The author is not clear about what will happen in each scene. • The complication may not be identified and the author is uncertain as to why the hero's mission has been set in motion. • The author may not be able to identify where each event will take place on his or her map. • The author is not able to identify how each conflict will be resolved. • The author does not know how the complication will be resolved in the climax. • The author cannot identify when and where each character will be introduced in the story. • There is no rise in tension or action as the story progresses to the climax.

PLOT LINE LISTENER RESPONSE

Readers should keep in mind that the response page should provide the writer with a variety of compliments that encourage, and with delicately worded suggestions for improvement. For the plot line, readers should write comments that reflect on the following qualities:

- Do you get a clear picture of the six scenes?
- Does the author know where each event will take place on the map?
- Is the complication clear? Does the author know why the hero's mission has been set in motion? And is the reason compelling enough to make *you* want to go along?
- Is the climax the most exciting and tension-filled scene in the story? Has the complication been resolved in the climax? Has the mission been solved?
- Does the author know what will happen in the final resolution?
- Is it clear when each character will be introduced in the story?

Name of Reader 1: _____

Comments: _____

_____

_____

_____

_____

Name of Reader 2: _____

Comments: _____

_____

_____

_____

_____

PLOT LINE LISTENER RESPONSE
(Continued)

Name of Reader 3: _____

Comments: _____

_____

_____

_____

_____

THE LINEAR PATH

One way to conceptualize a plot is to think in terms of a series of lines that head, in a rather crooked fashion, up to the peak of a mountain. This is a typical plot line for a story:

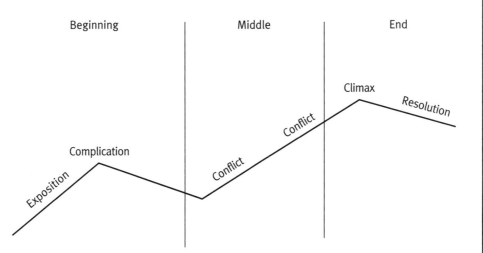

On this climbing line you will find an exposition, complication, two conflicts, the climax, and the resolution. The beginning comprises both the exposition and a complication, the middle contains the conflicts, and the end is both the exciting climax and resolution.

This plot line demonstrates a person's desire to go *out* in the world to make a difference, to slay an enemy, to accomplish a great deed. It also has a definitive beginning and a definitive end. Now let's explore the various points of interest along the path you'll be plotting.

THE BOLD BEGINNING

EXPOSITION

The exposition of a story shows where and when the story will take place. Most importantly, it exposes the reader to whom the story is about: your hero. Generally speaking, the exposition should provide the reader with a description of the setting and the everyday life of the main character. The exposition should open like a curtain on the action of characters on a stage. Start your story describing what the reader would see, hear, smell, and feel.

INITIAL ACTION SCENE

Sometimes during the exposition an initial action sequence is used. This action sequence is a great tool for hooking readers. Its job is to grab the readers' attention and draw them quickly into the story. Instead of starting the story off with an introductory description of where, when, and whom the story is about, the initial action scene sweeps readers up and immediately gets them involved in some exciting event. But in addition to giving us something enticing to follow, it should also reveal some insightful information about the main character and the world in which he or she lives.

COMPLICATION

The complication is the major turning point of the story. The complication disrupts the normal, everyday life of the main character. This event should take place relatively early in the story. You don't want to spend too much time exposing readers to the main character and the setting or they will probably lose interest. The complication is what kicks the story into high gear. It's the boot that propels the main character out from his life of ease and comfort into a world of chaos and conflict. The complication is the "big problem" that arises and absolutely must be resolved by the story's end. The complication holds your story together and gives it a sense of direction. It provides the motivation for the main character to go forward in her quest, taking big risks and facing grave danger during this most crucial moment of her life.

THE MERCURIAL MIDDLE

CONFLICTS

You must remember to make your middle *mercurial*. Middles that are mercurial are lively, witty, fast-talking, and likely to do the unexpected. And the best thing you can do to make your middle mercurial is to throw in a conflict or two. Conflicts are the turning points, twists, or hurdles that the hero must overcome. They are the devices that muddle the otherwise mundane life of the hero. They are the problems and difficulties the main character faces during his or her quest to solve the complication. Conflicts cause the plot to progress through a series of ups and downs. They bend the plot line into an interesting and exciting path for the hero.

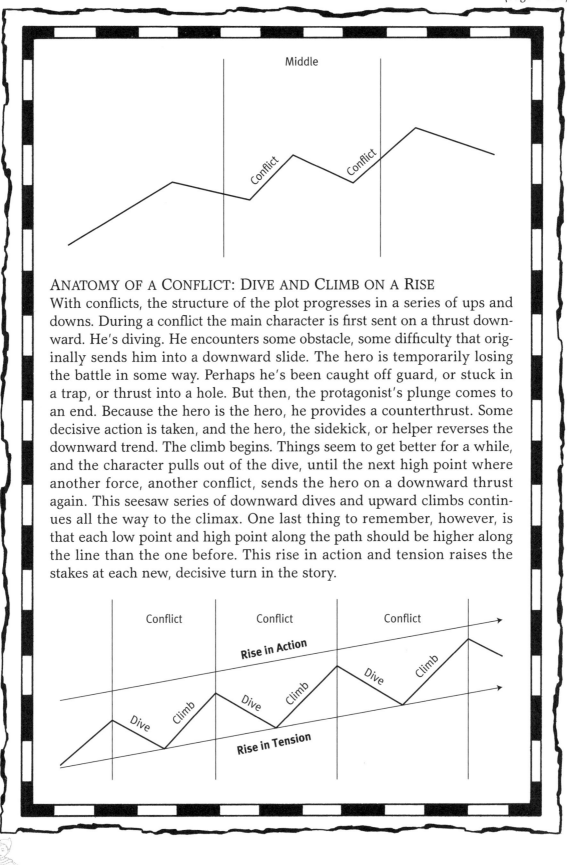

ANATOMY OF A CONFLICT: DIVE AND CLIMB ON A RISE

With conflicts, the structure of the plot progresses in a series of ups and downs. During a conflict the main character is first sent on a thrust downward. He's diving. He encounters some obstacle, some difficulty that originally sends him into a downward slide. The hero is temporarily losing the battle in some way. Perhaps he's been caught off guard, or stuck in a trap, or thrust into a hole. But then, the protagonist's plunge comes to an end. Because the hero is the hero, he provides a counterthrust. Some decisive action is taken, and the hero, the sidekick, or helper reverses the downward trend. The climb begins. Things seem to get better for a while, and the character pulls out of the dive, until the next high point where another force, another conflict, sends the hero on a downward thrust again. This seesaw series of downward dives and upward climbs continues all the way to the climax. One last thing to remember, however, is that each low point and high point along the path should be higher along the line than the one before. This rise in action and tension raises the stakes at each new, decisive turn in the story.

TYPES OF CONFLICT

If you're having difficulty deciding what conflicts your hero will encounter, here are a few ideas. There are many types of conflict, and they can easily arise from simple situations. Examine the following examples:

Person Versus Person

The person-to-person conflict is the most common type of conflict in any story or narrative. Here the hero or protagonist of the story meets up with someone and a problem unfolds. For our story of fantasy, it doesn't even have to be a "person." It could be some weird fantasy character or creature.

Person Versus Machine

Sometimes a character can have a problem with a machine that she needs to use in order to accomplish a task. The machine keeps breaking down. Or the character keeps using it the wrong way. In fantasy stories the "machine" could even be a wand or a staff that just doesn't seem to work right for some reason or another.

Person Versus Nature

A thunderstorm, a tornado, a hurricane, an earthquake, a dust devil, or a raging river: any of these natural phenomena can present interesting conflicts for the protagonist to solve. And in fantasy stories, there are even more dangerous and mysterious things to encounter—like an abyss to cross, or a talking tree to avoid!

Person Versus Self

Sometimes the main character of a story has to confront various internal issues. We call these *personality problems*. For example, maybe the hero is naïve, or overly optimistic, or pessimistic, or has a poor attitude, or has some issue to work through. Or perhaps the main character just keeps making the same mistake over and over again.

Person Versus Society

What if the society the character is living in isn't aware of a problem it has? For example, some people have lived in a society that hasn't always been aware of their special needs or challenges. Sometimes a character can help a society change its ways. The process of working out the person-versus-society conflict can be a very interesting, readable one.

THE ENTICING ENDING

CLIMAX

The climax is the biggest, most exciting scene in the story. This is where good finally confronts evil, where the final battle is waged. The climax is where the complication is solved. It's also the one scene where the hero has to make a major decision. Many exciting events, or conflicts, may have happened as the character tries to solve the conflict. But now—almost at the end of the story—there must be a major event where the hero finally makes a decision, performs an action, or reaches an understanding that grows out of all these conflicts: one way or another, during this scene, the complication is finally settled.

RESOLUTION

After the climax there's one last stage. This is the resolution or the finale. The resolution is usually very brief. It's the part of the story where the complication has already been solved. There's nothing left to fight for, so now the hero heads for home. People return to living normal lives again, but now, because of their heroic efforts, the protagonist and the sidekick and perhaps the helper and villain have learned something new about themselves and the world. And readers will finally know for sure what the theme, moral, point, or larger message of your story is.

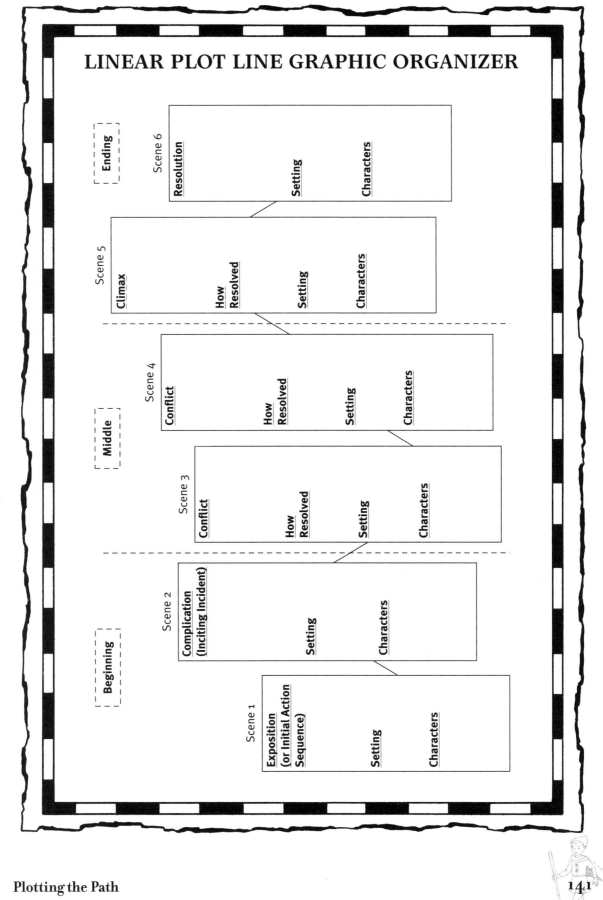

LINEAR PLOT LINE GRAPHIC ORGANIZER

Ending

Scene 6

Resolution

Setting

Characters

Scene 5

Climax

How Resolved

Setting

Characters

Middle

Scene 4

Conflict

How Resolved

Setting

Characters

Scene 3

Conflict

How Resolved

Setting

Characters

Beginning

Scene 2

Complication (Inciting Incident)

Setting

Characters

Scene 1

Exposition (or Initial Action Sequence)

Setting

Characters

MISSION IN MOTION: THE COMPLICATION

If you remember back to when you were working on your character descriptions, we learned that the main character must definitely have a motive. We also learned that this motivation is key to the plot because the motivated hero is what creates the action, what gets other people moving and reacting.

Why is the hero and his or her motivation key to the plot, you ask? Because the *motivation* is activated by the plot's *complication*. Therefore, special attention must be given to this first step on the protagonist's path. It is, after all, what sets the hero's mission in motion.

Remember: *Complication + Motivation = Mission in Motion.*

So, what exactly is it that your hero is after? Is it . . .

A ring?

A sword?

A crown?

A chalice?

An amulet?

A crystal ball?

A lad in a lair?

A damsel in distress?

An extraordinary elixir?

A book of enchantment?

A brother, sister, mother, or father who has been captured?

Winning a wife or husband?

Returning to a place visited in a dream?

Finding a home or getting a home back?

Helping someone recover his or her jewels or gold?

Saving a forest, a species of animal, or the human race?

What is it?

_____

_____

THE CIRCULAR PATH

There and back again is the very essence of fantasy. It's also the heart of adventure. If the hero or heroine of your fantasy story is to go there (wherever "there" is) and back again, the path, viewed from a heightened perspective, will resemble a circle.

The circle stands for wholeness, the experience of unity, and the theme of finding oneself. This circular plot line is a basic and ancient pattern found in the structure of many heroic stories.

Once you've learned the structure of this circular path, your job will be to revisit and perhaps re-create your protagonist's path with some fresh insights.

STEPS ALONG THE CIRCULAR PATH

STEP 1: GETTING THE CALL

The story begins with the hero somehow or another getting a call. Sometimes, the hero is lured away with the promise of a grand adventure. Treasures await and the hero must go. Or maybe someone is in trouble and must be saved. Other times, the hero has to take off for somewhere but doesn't really want to go. Such heroes may even be reluctantly carried away. At any rate, the hero leaves home on an urgent mission. He or she embarks on a perilous journey—a quest—to save the world from inevitable destruction. Step 1 on this circular path is getting the call.

STEP 2: PICKIN' UP A BUDDY AND A HELPER

Now the hero is about to experience a series of adventures and ordeals that will test his or her virtues and skills. But of course, all good heroes have a friend or two. And these friends—these sidekicks—being the good friends that they are, will volunteer to go along to help and support the hero's mighty quest. In addition to the trusty buddy, the hero usually picks up a helper of some sort. This helper is usually more than just a friend. The helper (the mentor) may be a strange, wise old man or woman, usually with powers and knowledge that surpass the ordinary.

THE CIRCULAR PATH
(Continued)

STEP 3: CROSSING OVER

After the hero gathers his sidekick and helper, he or she sets off and eventually runs smack dab into the entrance of a mysterious underworld: the threshold to the kingdom of the dark, a world where the hero and his or her friends have never before ventured. Usually, at the entrance to this passage to the underworld, there is a "shadow presence." And this shadow presence is guarding the threshold. At this point, the hero may defeat and destroy this power, or he may appease or satisfy it, in order to cross over into the kingdom of the dark. Sometimes, the hero slays a dragon guarding the entrance. Other times the hero offers an appealing charm to the guardian. And yet another way is when the hero is enticed into ingesting a potent elixir of some sort. Either way, in order for the story to continue, the hero, along with his or her sidekicks or buddies, must cross over into this dangerous, yet exciting, new realm.

STEP 4: TRIALS AND TRIBULATIONS

Beyond the threshold, the hero must survive a succession of tests, conflicts with strange forces, or struggles with weird characters. These ordeals severely threaten the hero and sidekick. Occasionally, the hero receives magical aid, advice, or powerful tools from the supernatural helper picked up before crossing over. And, of course, these tools are incredibly helpful for getting the hero out of at least one jam, and maybe more.

STEP 5: HITTING BOTTOM AND GETTING THE REWARD

Arriving at the *nadir* (lowest possible point) of the circle, the hero undergoes a supreme ordeal: a test of strength, smarts, and will. And even though it is the lowest point in the circle (meaning the hardest point on the journey), it is also the highest point of glory, the greatest moment of triumph. After a climatic struggle with the villain, or evil power, the quest or journey is over. The hero has gained the reward. This reward is sometimes called "the boon." There are several ways this boon can be received: The hero could fall in love; recover a powerful magical aid; be recognized by a father, creator, or king; reunite with a mother or old crone; acquire a new ability, power, or strength; or even gain a greater understanding of herself. In other words, the hero or heroine has been transformed!

THE CIRCULAR PATH
(Continued)

STEP 6: THE RETURN
Now that the task has been completed, the hero sets off for home. At the threshold of return (that scary place that once had to be crossed over) the hero reemerges from the mysterious underworld.

STEP 7: HEADING HOME
When the hero or heroine finally arrives home, he or she is greatly changed. Heroes and heroines have learned much about the world and themselves. So heading home is not just about getting them back to their old house. It's also about them looking at the home *inside* themselves, and learning something in return.

STEP 8: SAVING THE WORLD
The boon, the power, the instrument that the hero brought back restores the world. Things are returned to normal, but there is also a great recognition given to the hero for his or her efforts. And sometimes, the hero or heroine is crowned king or queen, and a new society and order form around them.

THE CIRCULAR PATH
(Continued)

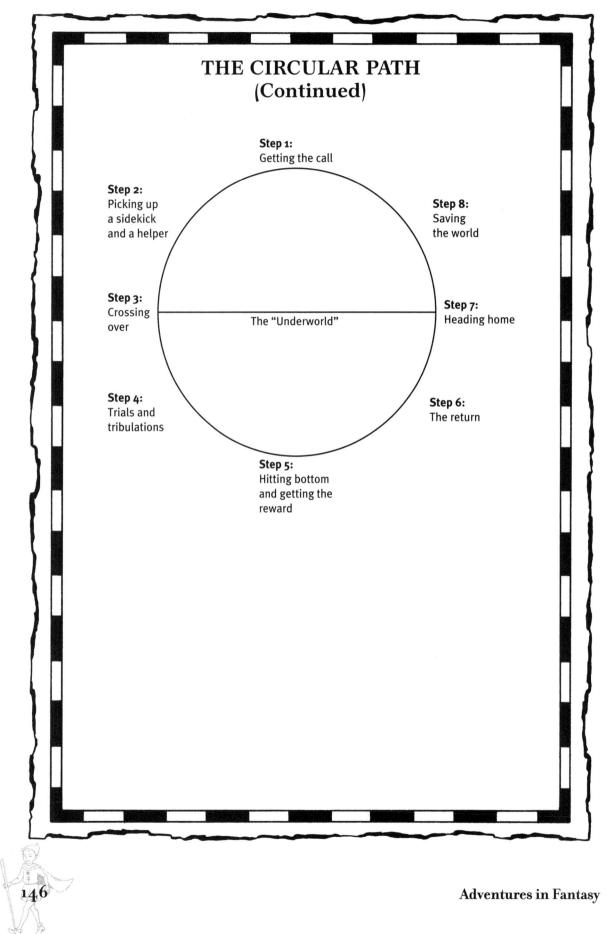

Step 1:
Getting the call

Step 2:
Picking up
a sidekick
and a helper

Step 8:
Saving
the world

Step 3:
Crossing
over

The "Underworld"

Step 7:
Heading home

Step 4:
Trials and
tribulations

Step 6:
The return

Step 5:
Hitting bottom
and getting the
reward

Adventures in Fantasy

THE CIRCULAR PATH
(Continued)

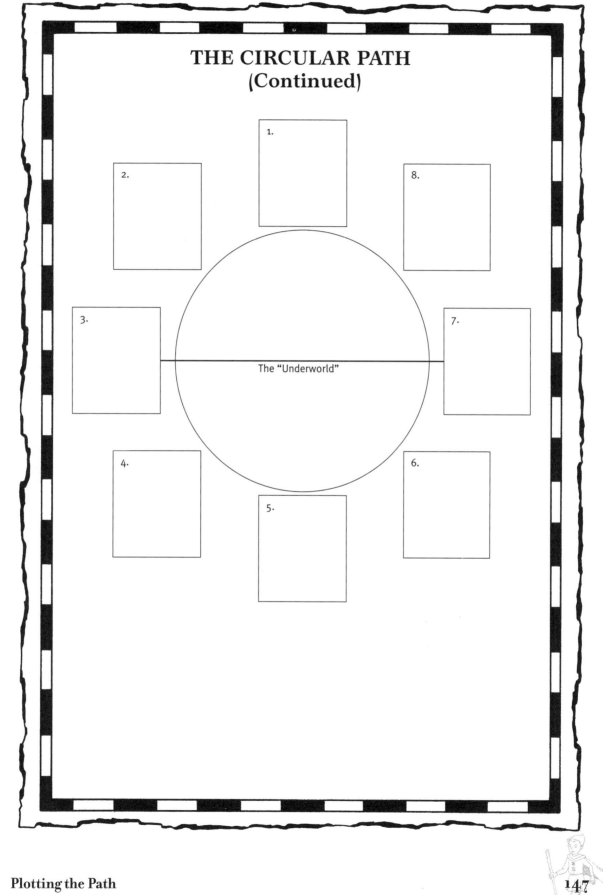

1.

2.

8.

3.

The "Underworld"

7.

4.

5.

6.

Plotting the Path

THEME THREAD: TRAVELING INWARD

So your hero is hiking along on his plot line, and you know what obstacles he's going to encounter, but do you know what changes are taking place inside of this character? How is he growing? What is he learning about himself or the world around him? Most characters in any good story learn and grow. They move upward in life and go deep within to learn something new about themselves. What is it that your hero or heroine is learning? Feeling? Becoming?

It is not enough just to plot your protagonist's footprints through your fantasyland. For your story to really have an impact on your readers, you must travel inward to explore the workings of the protagonist's mind and personality. For each step on your protagonist's path, identify the specific changes or "learnings" that are taking place inside the hero.

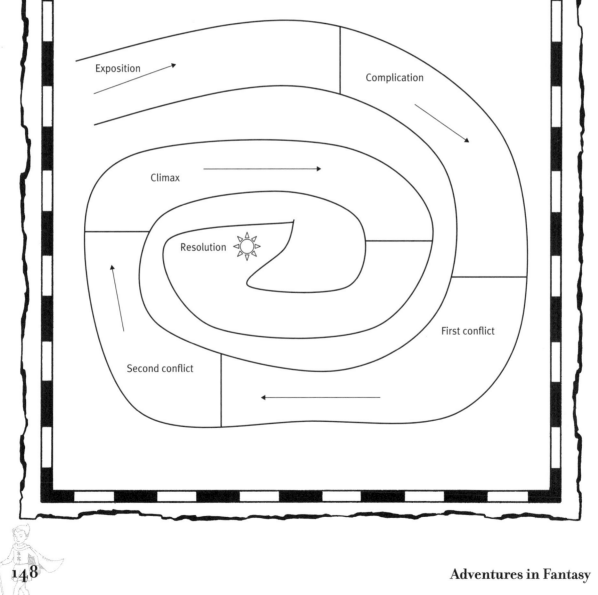

THEME THREAD: THE RESOLUTION

When deciding on a theme, it is helpful to know exactly *how* your story will end. To do this, you must focus on the resolution. When you can figure out how your story's complication will be resolved, you will know the theme, moral, point, or larger message of your story.

One thing you don't want to do, however, is to simply state your story's theme in the resolution, or ending. Nobody wants to hear you preaching about what you think! That's kind of like what fables do—they come with the moral of the story attached. Instead, you'll need to somehow *show* your readers the theme by way of the *actions* of your characters.

So, what do you want to see changed by the story's end? Each possible resolution will make a different point altogether. The goal is to find one that feels right to you—and to your main character. Remember, writing a story allows you to share your thoughts and feelings, and to express some part of your own view of the world. This means that the ending must somehow come out of your own truth. Hence, it must feel right and satisfying to you.

Knowing how your story will end will also help you know where it must begin. That is because the ending you intend will tell you what is important for the rest of the story. It will let you know what you want your readers to focus on right from the start.

Write down a few ideas on the next sheet about how you want your hero or heroine to solve the complication that got your story started. (Add more pages if you need to.) You don't need to know all the steps that your protagonist will take, but you should have some idea about how the resolution will feel. For example, your hero may not be able to change his circumstances, but he could change something inside himself. Or, yes, he could change the circumstances surrounding his life. Your hero could be victorious in the end, or he could be defeated, as well. Your hero could also make a new connection with someone in the story—possibly even the villain. Or your hero could just as easily turn away from someone. You decide.

THEME THREAD: THE RESOLUTION
(Continued)

_____

_____

_____

_____

_____

_____

_____

_____

_____

_____

_____

_____

_____

_____

_____

_____

_____

_____

_____

_____

_____

_____

_____

_____

_____

_____

_____

_____

Chapter Seven

Wording the Wonders

*Symbolic language is something that a young
child seems to understand almost viscerally;
metaphoric speech is the child's own speech,
though it is without analytic thought: a black
cat is called "Midnight," a white dog named
"Snowball"—immediate metaphors.*

—Jane Yolen

So far, if you've been following the sequence of lessons
provided in the book, students have had a chance to identify a
thought-provoking theme to thread through their tale. They've
created a mysterious fantasyland, drawn a map, and described, in
detail, various key locations of their story's setting. They've crafted
a complete cast of colorful, multidimensional characters and creatures. And they've designed a compelling plot with plenty of treacherous twists and turns. And still, they haven't written their story!
Do you think they're ready? Maybe. Maybe not.

Perhaps your students could use a little help with point of view,
transitions, "showing," or writing dialogue, or metaphors, similes,
alliteration, assonance, and even onomatopoeia. The pages in this
chapter are designed to equip your students with the words of wonder they'll need to make their stories engaging and entertaining to
read. Just imagine how many new magical literary aids, weapons,
and skills they will have acquired for their storytelling journey
when they're done here.

151

Before Beginning

Point of View

Prior to beginning the writing, students should decide what point of view they will use to tell their story. Once they decide, students will need to keep this point of view consistent throughout the story. All too often, for apparently no reason at all, students switch the point of view from which they are telling their story. It is highly recommended that our young, inexperienced writers choose either first-person or third-person limited point of view. Because it would be quite a huge undertaking for our young authors to take on the task of writing from a third-person omnipotent point of view, this perspective should be discouraged; there is simply too much information to get across. Students who choose a first-person point of view often place themselves as the protagonist in the story.

Transitions and Transitions of Time

Throughout their stories, students are going to have to communicate many different ideas and to link these ideas together into one coherent whole. At times, they're going to need to keep their readers oriented in terms of time and location; sometimes they'll need to help readers draw a conclusion or compare and contrast; other times they'll need to emphasize a particular point or sequence a series of events, or even summarize something that has been said. To do so effectively your students will need to be armed with a few transition words. Therefore, it is often helpful to pass out a copy of the transition words provided on the two worksheets. Review the transition words, provide examples of when certain ones might be most useful, and then allow your students to hold onto this resource to consult at a later time when the need arises. When students are busy revising and rewriting their stories, encourage them to take out these worksheets and consider adding one or two transition words when appropriate.

Story Showing

One of the most important things in telling a good story is not to tell, but rather to show. Showing the events of the story is much more detailed than telling them.

For example, here is an example of telling:

The janitor went into the classroom and cleaned it.

Showing, however, sounds a little different:

Tall, bald Janitor Joe wheeled his squeaky cart into the stuffy room. The cart was loaded with mops, brooms, rags, a huge trash can, and all sorts of stinky cleaning solvents. Janitor Joe snatched the broom off the cart and darted off in a flash, sweeping around all the desks. Janitor Joe had only ten minutes to spend in each classroom tonight, and he still had one hundred classrooms to go!

152

In showing, students will have to give the reader more of a play-by-play, step-by-step, breath-by-breath description of the events as they are taking place. The goal is to pick readers up and set them down in the scene so that they can see, hear, feel, smell, and maybe even taste ... everything going on. In story showing, the writer tries to paint a picture for the reader to enter.

When *showing*, students are often describing ...

- Action and events as they are taking place
- A character's looks, feelings, or movements
- A specific setting

The following two minilessons should get your classroom of writers' story *showing* off to a good start.

Show, Don't Tell: What Did They Do?

If a character is relieved he can grab his forehead, stare off into the distance, sit down with a thump, sigh, and say, "Whew!" If she's angry ... Well, I'm sure you can fill in the blanks. Can your students? If not, have individual students pick an emotion and ask that they act it out for the class. They can't say anything. They must act it out. On the worksheet provided, students can describe the emotional actions of each student actor. If writers want, they can embellish the actions of the student actor, showing more action than was provided.

Can You Fantasize? Prove It. Show It!

Here is an activity that gives students a chance to stretch their imaginations to describe a few fantasy settings, characters, objects, or events. To complete each selection, students will need to use as many exact words as possible. Exactly how does a fairy look "cute"? What do warlocks do if they're being "mean"? How is a gnome "helpful"? What makes a troll's lunch "gross"? Coach your students to use as many specific nouns, colorful adjectives, and precise, active verbs as possible.

Dynamic Dialogue

The goal here is to help students write dialogue that is dynamic, not dull. To do this, students need to know that dialogue is designed to help bring characters to life. Dialogue not only shows what a character thinks and feels but displays the character's personality and moods. Dialogue also demonstrates if a character is funny, silly, kind, angry, happy, or sad. Dynamic dialogue helps make the story come alive; it keeps the reader hooked and moves the story along. Use these minilessons to help your students write dynamic dialogue.

Speaker Tags

Students have a tendency to overuse the word "said" when writing dialogue. Most of the time, they aren't even aware of the alternative speaker tags available for their use. There are plenty of other choices. Before passing out the worksheet provided, ask your students to brainstorm words that could be used in place of the speaker tag "said." Ask them to think of words that might help project the feelings of characters when they're talking. Write their responses on the board. When your students have exhausted their supply, pass out the activity sheet and invite them to review the alternatives. Then have students group the alternatives according to the basic feelings provided in the textboxes.

Tagging Your Speakers

Once students have reviewed the alternative speaker tags provided and grouped them according to the basic feelings, invite them to begin assigning specific speaker tags to particular characters in their story. Later, when writing their narratives, they can refer back to this worksheet to pick and choose the speaker tags they might use for a specific character.

Quotations and Indents

Punctuating dialogue is always a challenge. Students often need to be reminded to use quotations properly, and to create a new paragraph and indent each time a new character speaks. Too often, students enclose an entire conversation between two or more characters all in one paragraph! This can be incredibly difficult to read and decipher.

Say Do ... Do Say ... Say Do Say ... Talk and Feel ... Think and Talk

Have you ever read a student's narrative that includes two or more characters standing still, doing absolutely nothing, except talking, talking, talking away? They don't move, they don't think, and they don't feel ... anything! Students need to know that if they want to keep their readers engaged and capable of visualizing what is happening in the story, they will need to provide more than just the spoken words and speaker tags of the characters conversing in the scene. This minilesson is designed to guide students to include the movements, thoughts, and feelings of characters while they are engaged in dialogue. Remember, we want the dialogue to be dynamic, not dull!

Figurative Language

If our goal is to get kids thinking and writing beyond the literal realm, then fantasy is the perfect genre for moving a young writer's mind into the figurative. Fantasy is ripe with opportunity to make "things" come alive. Moreover, mastering metaphors is more easily done in the magical world of fantasy. Where else could a writer spend so much time musing away mastering the art of calling one thing another? Use the lessons provided here and watch your student writers create more vivid pictures in their readers' minds than ever before.

Personification

A chair that hugs. A tree that stretches its limbs. Personally, I like personification. It gives students a chance to become what Tolkien called *sub-creators*, making various inanimate parts of their world come alive, act, move, and communicate, just like humans. The act of personification is ancient. Just think of how many objects and natural processes have been personified into gods? But in these modern times, well, do we practice personification readily? Don't let the ancient art of personification slip into the swallowing sands of literalism. Figure it out. Figurative language is in!

Similes

Second comes similes. Fantasy provides an ample source of opportunity to enchant one's words by saying one thing is "like" or "as" another. The first student worksheet provides a few fun fantasy similes, and then invites writers to complete a series of sentence stems to create their own similes. The next student worksheet provides several word groupings (objects, concepts, feelings, beings, and so on) and then challenges the students to pair the different things once they can determine a similarity that facilitates the creation of a simile. With the practice provided here, students should remember the writing device, and use it to enchant the wording of the wonders their heroes will encounter in their stories.

Be a Master of Metaphor

The greatest thing by far is to be a master of metaphor. It is the one thing that cannot be learned from others; and it is also a sign of genius, since a good metaphor implies an intuitive perception of the similarity in dissimilars.

—Aristotle

Despite what Mr. Aristotle thought about this one thing that students cannot learn from another, we're still going for it! Students *will* become *masters of metaphor!* They will see the similarity in the dissimilars. Are we psyched yet? I figured we'd need all the motivation we could get to buck Mr. Aristotle and begin the teaching of metaphors. We *will* prove the famous philosopher wrong; however, it will be a difficult task. To begin, make sure you realize that your students' experiences are going to determine their metaphors. Ultimately, they will need to look for the dissimilars and their similarities within their own lives to become true masters of metaphor. Thus, it is our job to inspire our students to look around, and deep inside, to identify the dissimilars and their similarities.

The purpose of the activities provided here is to get students' minds looking at dissimilars, and then match them as they realize their similarities.

This practice will help get students familiar with looking for the similarities in the dissimilars, and also fine-tune their intuitive perceptions. This will help them identify a metaphor when it appears. When they can do this readily, they will be true masters of metaphor.

The Sounds of Words

Students need to know that good writers often choose words not just for what they mean, or to convey a particular thought, but also for the simple enjoyment of the sounds they make. The lessons provided here will help tune your students' ears to the sounds of words. By incorporating a little alliteration, assonance, and onomatopoeia, students will begin to stretch their imaginations to craft combinations of words that will make their writing more pleasant and fun to read.

How About a Little Alliteration?

One really fun way to start this minilesson is to try creating sentences that incorporate students' names in fun alliterative phrases. For example: *Zany Zachary zoomed around the zoo on a zippy zebra, yelling, "Zowie, zowie!"* This usually captures their attention, and in a very short time, effectively teaches the writing device as well. Of course, if you start using student names to provide examples of alliteration, you're going to have to give a few students the chance to do the same with your name, too. Then, after everybody has had their fun, pass out the worksheet provided, and ask students to do the same thing with the characters in their story.

The Land of Assonance

Assonance is a slightly harder skill to acquire than the preceding one. Vowels in the middle of words, repeated in succession, are more difficult to produce than consonants at the beginning of words, as in alliteration. Getting students started with names is a great way to create the sounds of assonance. The words don't actually have to make much sense, so students can concentrate solely on the sounds of the words. Later, they can try to apply the skill on *real* words, in coherent phrases or sentences.

Whack! Bang! Ping! Onomatopoeia

Action! That's what we're looking for in onomatopoeia. First, invite your students to review the additional onomatopoeia words provided. By then students should have a good idea of what sorts of sounds they could possibly incorporate in their stories. Then have them choose an action or a character, and challenge them to create a sentence that uses onomatopoetic words. Students will have to visualize that specific character doing something within some scene in their story. Hopefully, later on they'll be able to incorporate those words and sentences in their story.

POINT OF VIEW

The point of view of a story is the position from which a story is told. It is where the storyteller or narrator is in relation to the story. When you write a story, you must be consistent in the point of view you choose. There are several points of view to choose from.

FIRST PERSON

The narrator is one of the characters, often the main character, in the story. The narrator or speaker uses the first-person pronouns *I, me, my, we, us,* and *our* to describe what he or she says, does, and thinks. Although the actions and words of other characters are described, only the thoughts of the narrator may be described. Use the first person "I" in your writing when you want your readers to feel close to and identify with the narrating character.

THIRD PERSON

The story is told from a point of view outside the action of the story. The narrator is not a character in the story but is instead an outside observer.

THIRD-PERSON LIMITED

This point of view requires the narrator to tell the story from only one character's perspective. As the reader follows this character through the story, they only know the internal thoughts and feelings of this one person. As for the other characters, you will have to show the reader who they are by describing only their actions, movements, dialogue, and appearance.

THIRD-PERSON OMNIPOTENT

If you are omnipotent, then you possess complete, unlimited, or universal power and authority. If you're writing a story from this point of view, it means that you know what is going on inside the heads of each and every character. And not only do you know as the narrator, but your writing demonstrates this knowledge. Basically, it means that readers get to know what everybody is thinking and feeling.

POINT OF VIEW
(Continued)

Circle the point of view from which you will tell your fantasy story:

First Person   Third-Person Limited   Third-Person Omnipotent

Now write at least one sentence that describes your hero doing something. Use the point of view you have chosen.

_____

_____

_____

_____

_____

_____

_____

_____

_____

_____

_____

_____

_____

_____

_____

TRANSITIONS

Transitions are key words that provide a signal to show the order of important events or to connect one idea to another. Transitions are often used at the beginning of a paragraph or sentence. Their job is to link one paragraph or sentence to another. All good writers use transitions to keep their readers focused. Use the following transitions for the purposes specified:

To link thoughts

again	also	and	so
besides	further	furthermore	in addition
last	next	likewise	moreover

To compare ideas

also	as well as	in the same way	likewise
similarly	resembling	too	both
just as	like		

To contrast

after all	although	on the other hand	however
nevertheless	on the contrary	in contrast	yet
but	even though	otherwise	still
while			

To show sequence and time

after	immediately	before	during
earlier	meanwhile	at the same time	while
at once	first, second,	simultaneously	last
yesterday	third, etc.	this morning	today
tomorrow	the day before	at that very moment	next
tonight			

TRANSITIONS
(Continued)

To show cause and effect

accordingly	because	as a result
due to	then	thus
therefore	consequently	since

To emphasize

indeed	in fact	to be sure	truly
undoubtedly	without a doubt	no doubt about it	surely

To summarize

consequently	to sum up	in conclusion	as a result
in closing	finally	ultimately	in summary
last	lastly	therefore	

TRANSITIONS OF TIME

Quick! Your characters are going to be on a trail. They're going to be traveling. Time will pass! In what order will these things happen? Will they happen . . . at that moment? Suddenly? Before? During? After? After *what?* Do a quick write. Write out a sequence of events that will take place on your hero's trail. Or describe an experience your hero might have over time. Don't think too hard. Just let the ideas flow. Make no judgments. Just make sure you use a few transitions of time.

Transitions of Time

about
after
at
before
during
first
second
third
then
until
meanwhile
today
tomorrow
tonight
yesterday
next
soon
later
finally
as soon as
now
when
while
at that moment
suddenly
simultaneously

(Continue on another sheet of paper, if necessary.)

SHOW, DON'T TELL: WHAT DID THEY DO?

Sometimes writers tell the reader how a character is feeling. That's pretty good, actually. Readers need to know how a character is feeling. However, it's even better if readers discover how a character is feeling by *seeing* what that character is doing. Don't tell readers that some character is angry or sad or happy. Rather, show them what that character does so that they will be able to draw their own conclusion about the character's feelings.

Write a paragraph describing what a character would *do* if he or she were feeling . . .

Excited: _____

_____

_____

_____

_____

_____

_____

Sad: _____

_____

_____

_____

_____

_____

Exhausted: _____

_____

_____

_____

_____

_____

_____

Adventures in Fantasy

SHOW, DON'T TELL: WHAT DID THEY DO?
(Continued)

Disgusted: _____

_____

_____

_____

_____

_____

Angry: _____

_____

_____

_____

_____

_____

_____

Happy: _____

_____

_____

_____

_____

_____

_____

Bored: _____

_____

_____

_____

_____

_____

Wording the Wonders

SHOW, DON'T TELL: WHAT DID THEY DO?
(Continued)

In pain: _____

_____

_____

_____

_____

_____

Scared: _____

_____

_____

_____

_____

_____

_____

Nervous: _____

_____

_____

_____

_____

_____

Relieved: _____

_____

_____

_____

_____

_____

Adventures in Fantasy

CAN YOU FANTASIZE? PROVE IT. SHOW IT!

Rewrite the following sentences, changing them from telling sentences to showing sentences. *Fantasize! See* it in your mind. Then write it on the paper!

The fairy is cute. _____

_____

_____

_____

_____

The warlock was so mean. _____

_____

_____

_____

_____

The castle looked abandoned. _____

_____

_____

_____

_____

The gnome was very helpful. _____

_____

_____

_____

_____

It was an exciting battle. _____

_____

_____

_____

_____

The princess was beautiful. _____

_____

_____

_____

_____

The elf cleaned his house. _____

_____

_____

_____

_____

Troll lunches are gross. _____

_____

_____

_____

_____

The wizard had a great outfit. _____

_____

_____

_____

_____

It was a magnificent sword. _____

_____

_____

_____

_____

The dragon was destructive. _____

_____

_____

_____

_____

Adventures in Fantasy

SPEAKER TAGS

All writers use speaker tags, phrases such as *said Morty* and *she asked* to let their readers know who is speaking. "Said" *can* be overused, however. Therefore, you may want to consider using other words in place of "said":

answered	asked	replied	exclaimed	explained
declared	remarked	added	advised	commented
reported	suggested	begged	inquired	admitted
agreed	announced	argued	claimed	confided
encouraged	implored	requested	asserted	responded
stated	noted	objected	proclaimed	reasoned

Some speaker tags show a speaker's feelings, tone of voice, or mood, and at the same time make the dialogue more interesting. Check out these substitutes:

screamed	shouted	slurred	moaned	screeched
mumbled	groaned	whined	growled	hissed
whispered	stuttered	cried	chuckled	scoffed
yelled	grumbled	laughed	sneered	snapped
bellowed	stammered	snarled	muttered	demanded
coughed	hollered	squealed	shrieked	sighed
wailed	urged	gasped	croaked	giggled
boasted	hooted	insisted	pleaded	commanded
nagged	ordered	scolded	sobbed	threatened
babbled	bargained	bragged	warned	vowed
taunted	sputtered	lectured	grunted	complained
grumbled	wept	howled	blared	fumed
quivered	pleaded	trembled	soothed	yelped
joked	sighed	begged	threatened	lied

Now take these tags and group them according to the feelings shown in the following boxes.

SPEAKER TAGS
(Continued)

Sad	Pain	Anger

Fear	Joy	Love

Desire

Adventures in Fantasy

TAGGING YOUR SPEAKERS

Pick any character you have and then think of which one of the preceding feelings and corresponding speaker tags would be fitting for them. If you have a sidekick, for example, which speaker tag would that character most likely use? Try to think of a specific situation they would be in, imagine how they would feel, and then choose the appropriate feeling and speaker tag. Would the character be sad, mad, scared, or happy? Would he wail, mutter, shriek, or bellow? And, finally, if you can think of exactly what he would say during a certain situation, write that in the last column.

Character Type (Hero, Helper, Sidekick, Conflict Character, Villain)	Character Name	Speaker Tags the Character Would Most Likely Use	Using a Speaker Tag, What Exactly Would the Character Say?

QUOTATIONS AND INDENTS

When writing narratives, a big portion of your story is going to include dialogue. When writing dialogue, there are a few basic rules that all writers must follow.

Rule 1: Punctuation

The first rule to keep in mind concerns your use of quotation marks. Quotation marks must always be used to enclose the exact words of the speaker. Well, that may be a simple enough rule to follow, but consider this: Should the periods, commas, question marks, and exclamation marks go inside or outside of the quotation marks? If you said inside, you're right! For example:

"Watch out for the dragon!" shouted Pormon the elf.

"May I use your trusty sword to defend myself?" asked Tanka.

"Most definitely," said Pormon as he quickly handed his sword to Tanka.

"Thank you." Tanka raised the sword to prepare for the onslaught of the dragon.

Notice how all the punctuation marks (exclamation mark, question mark, comma, and period) are all inside the quotation marks?

Rule 2: Paragraphs

The second rule to follow when writing dialogue is that you must absolutely, positively begin a new paragraph each and every time a new person starts speaking. For example, if two or more people are having a conversation, even if someone speaks just one word, a new paragraph must be created. Therefore, you must skip down to the next line, indent, and then write the speaker's words. Take a good look at the following example:

"How do you know about all of this?" asked Lazarus. "Well, I come from the Pleiades," said Zanadar. "You see, we Pleiadians are responsible for maintaining your Earth's planetary grid." "Yeah, right," scoffed a sarcastic Armando. "You guys are in charge of it, huh?" "Okay," interrupted Kyle, now anxious to get busy. "So how are we supposed to create this vortex?" "Have any of you ever heard of Metatron's Cube?" asked Zanadar. Everyone shook their heads and looked around at each other in confusion. "What do they teach you people in school these days!" shouted the Pleiadian. "This is one of the most important informational systems in the universe, one of the basic creation

Adventures in Fantasy

QUOTATIONS AND INDENTS
(Continued)

patterns of existence!" Zanadar shook his head in disbelief. "Well, excuse us for not knowing, old timer," said Armando. "Don't let it worry ya' little buddy," said Zanadar, cracking a smile.

Obviously, this is an example of the *wrong* way to break up this dialogue into paragraphs! In this one paragraph, there are actually four people talking.

Now take a look at the very same conversation. You'll notice that there is no longer just one paragraph, but rather ... nine!

"How do you know about all of this?" asked Lazarus.

"Well, I come from the Pleiades," said Zanadar. "You see, we Pleiadians are responsible for maintaining your Earth's planetary grid."

"Yeah, right," scoffed a sarcastic Armando. "You guys are in charge of it, huh?"

"Okay," interrupted Kyle, now anxious to get busy. "So how are we supposed to create this vortex?"

"Have any of you ever heard of Metatron's Cube?" asked Zanadar.

Everyone shook their heads and looked around at each other in confusion.

"What do they teach you people in school these days!" shouted the Pleiadian. "This is one of the most important informational systems in the universe, one of the basic creation patterns of existence!" Zanadar shook his head in disbelief.

"Well, excuse us for not knowing, old timer," said Armando.

"Don't let it worry ya' little buddy," said Zanadar, cracking a smile.

This is obviously the correct way to use paragraphs in this conversation. Make sure *you* also create a new paragraph and indent each time a new person talks.

SAY DO … DO SAY … SAY DO SAY …
TALK AND FEEL … THINK AND TALK

SAY DO … DO SAY … SAY DO SAY

Characters don't just stand there and talk. They're *doing* something! But what? What are they doing? Are they scratching? Yawning? Rubbing their eyes? Walking in circles? Running up a flight of stairs? You must decide!

For example:

> "Let's get out of here!" said Joe. "The troll is coming!"

… isn't nearly as effective as …

> Joe took off running down the hill. "Let's get out of here! The troll is coming!"

You can do/say (place the action before the words) …

> Andy took off his helmet and scratched his head. "Why are we here, at Murk Water Swamp? I thought we were headed for the Mystical Mountains."

Or say/do …

> "Why are we here at Murk Water Swamp? I thought we were headed for the Mystical Mountains." Andy took off his helmet and scratched his head.

Or say/do/say …

> "Why are we here at Murk Water Swamp?" asked Andy while taking off his helmet and scratching his head. "I thought we were headed for the Mystical Mountains."

TALK AND FEEL … THINK AND TALK

Characters also have feelings when they are talking. Sometimes it's good to let us know what those feelings are …

> "Hail," replied the King, anxious to make a good impression.

Characters have internal thoughts as well.

> Joey wondered if the ogre was going to eat all the food in *his* backpack. "What do you say we get moving? We've got a long way to go."

PERSONIFICATION

Personification gives human characteristics, abilities, or qualities to non-human things. Personification is when an author writes about a thing as if it were human.

Hmm! Interestingly enough, there are plenty of nonhuman things with the potential to exhibit humanlike characteristics in stories of fantasy. Trees, mountains, clouds, rivers, plains, deserts, winds, rain—all can come "alive" in the world of fantasy. So there must be plenty of opportunity to add a little personification to your story. Perhaps your story's setting, once it becomes personified, can begin fighting back in some way. Things can come alive and provide all kinds of challenges or obstacles for any one of your characters.

Here are a few examples of personification:

The rain slapped Luella and Zianna in the face as they descended the hill on their way to the Dinador.

The throne groaned under the ogre's great weight.

The chariot wheels screamed around the turn.

Fear lived with the king in his castle.

To get started, all you need to do is to have a nonhuman thing *do* something that only a human can do. For example: What could the wind do? How about: *The wind wailed in the night.*

Now it's your turn. See if you can find some humanlike thing that each of the following objects could do.

What could a *cloud* do? _____

_____

What could a *mountain* do? _____

_____

What could a *river* do? _____

_____

What could a *tree* do? _____

_____

PERSONIFICATION
(Continued)

What could a *castle* do? _____

_____

What could a *cave* do? _____

_____

What could a *sword* do? _____

_____

What could an *arrow* do? _____

_____

What could a *cloak* do? _____

_____

What could a *mirror* do? _____

_____

What could a *desert* do?_____

_____

What could the *sea* do? _____

_____

What could a *swamp* do? _____

_____

What could a *shield* do? _____

_____

What could a *book of spells* do? _____

_____

Adventures in Fantasy

SIMILES, PART I

Similes are figures of speech that draw a comparison between two different things. Similes use the words "like" and "as" to compare these two different things.

Here are a few examples to get you going:

The troll was as ugly as a toad.

The castle was as quiet as a tomb.

Ranzak's mind was like a cold, dark cave.

Yuknuk, the troll, was as tall as a mountain.

The dancing elves swayed like trees in the wind.

The princess fainted and fell like a feather to the ground.

The dwarfs were crushed like ants below the flat feet of the giants.

The blood in Vindor's vindictive veins ran quick and cold as an icy river.

Now it's your turn. See if you can turn these sentence stems into similes:

The wizard's pointed hat was crushed as flat as a _____

The magical sword was as light as a _____

The small fairy was as brave as a _____

The goblin's teeth were as sharp as _____

The princess was as pretty as _____

The gallant soldier fought like _____

The unicorn was as swift as a _____

The giant was as gentle as _____

The sorcerer's bed was as soft as a _____

Heading down the steps into the deep cavern, the dwarf scurried along like _____

Hearing the dragon's roar was like _____

SIMILES, PART II

Here is another way to create some similes. Try choosing a word from Column One and relate it in some way to another word from Column Two. Find some connection, and then create a sentence with a simile in it. Don't forget to use "like" or "as."

Column One	Column Two
light	bat
white	whistle
cole	doorknob
clean	sheet
blind	feather
dumb	ice

1. _____
2. _____
3. _____
4. _____
5. _____
6. _____

Column One	Column Two
proud	tack
good	pie
sly	gold
please	fox
sharp	peacock
easy	punch

1. _____
2. _____
3. _____
4. _____
5. _____
6. _____

Adventures in Fantasy

SMILES, PART II
(Continued)

Column One	Column Two
wiggly	flea
stubborn	nails
playful	mule
hard	kitten
strong	worm
tiny	ox

1. _____
2. _____
3. _____
4. _____
5. _____
6. _____

Column One	Column Two
quick	arrow
graceful	dog
smart	gazelle
straight	fiddle
fit	wink
sick	whip

1. _____
2. _____
3. _____
4. _____
5. _____
6. _____

BE A MASTER OF METAPHOR, PART I

The word *metaphor* comes from the Greek words *meta*, which means a passing over, or a going from one place to another, and *phorein*, which means to move or to carry. Therefore, the job of a metaphor is to basically move the reader's mind from one place to another! Metaphors make it easy for readers to cross boundaries that would otherwise be closed.

Metaphors are imaginative kinds of comparisons. Saying that someone is a snake is an example of a metaphor. Metaphors simply state that one thing *is* another. And unlike similes, which compare two things by using *like* or *as*, metaphors do the comparing without using either of those two words.

When comparing one thing to another by creating a metaphor, you are not literally representing real things by saying that one thing is actually another thing; rather, you are speaking *figuratively*. Figurative language refers to words or groups of words that stand for more than their literal meaning. Writers use figurative language to create vivid pictures in readers' minds.

Writers can use metaphors in almost any part of their writing, but to do so effectively the audience must be familiar with the two things being compared. Therefore, writers must rely on the experience of their audience to understand and appreciate the metaphor. But authors must rely on the ability to put together or associate two different "remembered experiences" and take readers from one directly to the other. If you can do this, you will be exhibiting signs of genius! You will be ... a *master of metaphorrrrrr!*

Here are a few simple examples:

The witch's face was a prune.

The sick fairy was a grouchy grizzly.

The elf was a busy bee working in his garden.

The castle was covered in a blanket of darkness.

The orc soldiers were a standing row of dominoes waiting to fall.

The line of goblins leading into the cave was a slithering serpent.

The gnome was a quiet mouse skittering through the darkened tunnel.

The dwarfs were gophers burrowing from place to place deep in their caverns.

Now it's time to create a few metaphors of your own. There are several ways to do this.

METAPHORS FOR CHARACTERS

You could take a character from your story and try to compare his appearance, actions, or personality to something else. Think about it. Pick a character. What does he look like? Does his face remind you of a certain fruit? How does he move? Do his actions remind you of a particular insect? What about his personality? Does he have the disposition of a special animal? Take a moment to think, and then write your metaphors here:

_____

_____

_____

_____

METAPHORS FOR LANDMARKS

You could also try to describe how a particular landmark on your map looks by comparing it with a specific human or animal body part. Take a moment to think, and then write your metaphors here:

_____

_____

_____

_____

METAPHORS CREATED FROM A DIFFERENT PERSPECTIVE

What if you could view an object from the perspective of a small, crawling insect, a flying dragon, or a tall giant? Would that object look or feel like something else altogether?

Try to view some object through the eyes of another creature. Most likely, that creature will have an entirely different and unique relationship with, or perspective on, that object. For example, what would a hummingbird think of a flower? What would an ant think of a big rock? What would a cricket think of a patch of grass?

Try to create a few metaphors using the following sentence formats:

A _____ is a _____ to a _____.

A _____ is a _____ to a _____.

An _____ is a _____ for a _____.

An _____ is a _____ for a _____.

Wording the Wonders

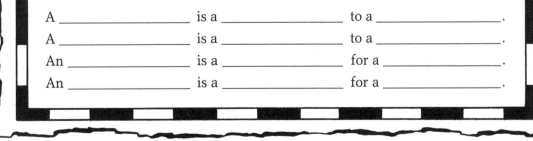

BE A MASTER OF METAPHOR, PART II

See if you can find the matching items from the two columns in each set to create a metaphor. Write each metaphor in a complete sentence on another sheet of paper.

Column One	Column Two
scream	pigpen
dancing elf	a cold, wet fish
branches of a tree	open container
cloud	garbage can
a goblin's handshake	spinning top
grass stalks	witch's spindly fingers
child's mind	blaring siren
dwarf's bedroom	cotton candy
villain's mouth	marble pillars

Column One	Column Two
life	silent, slithering snake
a giant's footsteps	blanket of diamonds
storm	searchlight
spiked hair	bobbing cork
thief	peals of thunder
sunshine	roaring dragon
dragon's eyes	journey
stars	a warm, yellow comforter
small boat	forest

Adventures in Fantasy

HOW ABOUT A LITTLE ALLITERATION?

Alliteration is the repetition of an initial consonant sound in words that are close together. Writers use alliteration to have fun and entertain. It also helps them achieve different moods. Alliteration is most often used in poetry, but it can also be used in fiction.

Here's a good way to get the alliteration flowing. Pick any character. Let's say you've got a helper named Grindor. Well, Grindor can be a grumpy, grouchy wizard. And he's always grimacing, growling, and grunting. But sometimes, when something grand happens, Grindor occasionally grins and becomes quite gracious. Obviously, the consonant blend "gr" was the example of alliteration.

See? That wasn't so difficult. Now you try. Pick a character and then start searching for words that alliterate.

Character Name	Alliteration Words	Create a Sentence Using as Many Alliteration Words as Possible

THE LAND OF ASSONANCE

Have you ever heard of Lassonance, Ragassonance, or Sapassonance? No, you say? Well, they were brothers. And they lived a long time ago in the Land of Assonance. You don't believe it? Well, okay, not really. But in another story there *were ...*

Dw*alin* and B*alin*,

    K*ili* and F*ili*,

        D*ori*, N*ori*, and *Ori*,

            Oin and Gl*oin*,

                Bif*ur*, Bof*ur*, and Bomb*ur*,

                    and Thor*in.*

    J.R.R. Tolkien must have had a barrel of fun creating the names of his thirteen dwarves in *The Hobbit.* When he put together the unlucky number of names, he was using a dash of assonance. Assonance is when words with similar vowel or consonant sounds are placed close to each other in a sentence. These sounds usually come in the *middle syllable* of a three-syllable word, or as the *end syllable* of any other word. Assonance is kind of like alliteration. Alliteration, if you remember, is when consonant or vowel sounds are repeated at the *beginning* of the word.

    So, join in on the fun Tolkien must have had and try creating a few new funny names of your own, while also using a dash of assonance. Then see if you can stream these new "words" together in a sentence.

    When you master the skill of assonance, however, you will need to venture further than using it in the creation of new names lined up all in a row. When you have mastered the skill of assonance, you will be able to d*anc*e, rom*anc*e, and beat the p*ants* off of any ... dumb **ants**. Huh? That's assonance, silly!

    And then there was C*uk*, Can*uk*, and Canacan*uk*. Y*uk*, y*uk*, y*uk*! They were trolls from the Land of An*uk*. What? You haven't heard of these characters, either?

    Now it's your turn. Try to create a few names using the writing device called assonance. Write the names on the back of this sheet.

WHACK! BANG! PING! ONOMATOPOEIA

Boom! Crash! Nick Rankin and his pet dragon Yuri ran for cover as giant flaming meteors started to hit the wooden roof on Nick's house.

—Student Joshua Villaruz, *The Time of Mini Russia*

"Booming" and "crashing" are onomatopoetic words. When you use *onomatopoeia,* you use words that imitate the sound made by or connected with the thing to which you refer. Use onomatopoeia to give your writing pleasant sounds for the ears to hear.

Check out these onomatopoetic words. Use as many as you can to create phrases, or sentences, about interesting things that creatures or characters in your story may do. For example: *Whish-whoosh, whish-whoosh beat the dragon's wings as he soared through the air.* Now it's your turn!

sizzle	whack	meow	baa	clink	tinkle
buzz	bang	snort	sputter	rattle	chomp
hum	wheeze	beep	blink	boom	splat
bowwow	chirp	chug	clang	clap	screech
clatter	zoom	click	yawn	cluck	howl
whistle	cough	tap	snap	ping	gobble
plop	crash	drip	fizz	splash	zip
squeal	munch	quack	rip	slam	thump
snip	moo	gurgle	slap	hiss	hush
squish	grate	creak	flip	flop	smash
moan	roar	smack	splash	ring	slurp
tick-tock	rustle	swish	thud	pop	tweet
pitter-patter	jabber	chime	squeak	whir	snap
crackle	crunch	murmur	mumble	honk	groan
whish	whiz	whoosh			

Wording the Wonders

WHACK! BANG! PING! ONOMATOPOEIA
(Continued)

Write a sentence that describes the sounds heard at a specific setting on your map:

_____

_____

_____

_____

_____

_____

Write a sentence that describes the sounds made by a character's actions:

_____

_____

_____

_____

_____

_____

Adventures in Fantasy

Chapter Eight

Sketching the Scene

It is one of the most interesting pictures he ever made, and one of the most meticulously drawn. It brings the Hobbit village to life, and directly influenced the description of Hobbiton in The Lord of the Rings, *where Bagshot Row, the Old Grange, and the party tree (in the field just below Bag-End), among other details, are first mentioned in the text.*

—Wayne G. Hammond and Christina Scull, describing Tolkien's drawing of *The Hill: Hobbiton Across the Water*

What is the most basic unit of any story? Is it the sentence? A paragraph? A chapter? Nope. None of these. It's the scene: the fundamental component of all fiction. In a scene, a problem is presented for one or more of the characters. The characters deal with the problem. And dealing with the problem reveals something about each character while also moving the story along.

A scene can take as little as a sentence or two, or it can go on for pages. A scene is complete when a presented conflict has been resolved, or has caused the hero to plunge deeper into trouble. This shouldn't mean ever-increasing doom, but it does mean that even if the scene ends favorably for the characters involved, this triumph should only lead to a more traumatic scene yet to come. Remember, as a story progresses its tension is supposed to rise.

Okay, so how do you drive this point home for your students, so that they will understand that their writing needs to progress from scene to scene? I've discovered that before the writing begins, it is often helpful to allow students an opportunity to illustrate the scenes of their story. Doing so helps bring each scene and eventually the entire story to life. Once students start to draw, the details of each scene begin to emerge, and this supplies the help they'll need to fully describe the setting, character actions, and dialogue that each scene typically requires.

On Camazotz, in *A Wrinkle in Time,* by Madeleine L'Engle

To get students comfortable with thinking of their story as one scene happening at a time, I like to expose them to the passage from *A Wrinkle in Time,* by Madeleine L'Engle, that describes what Meg, Calvin, and Charles see when they first arrive on the planet Camazotz:

> Below them the town was laid out in harsh angular patterns. The houses in the outskirts were all exactly alike, small square boxes painted gray. Each had a small, rectangular plot of lawn in front, with a straight line of dull-looking flowers edging the path to the door. Meg had a feeling that if she could count the flowers there would be exactly the same number for each house. In front of all the houses children were playing. Some were skipping rope, some were bouncing balls. Meg felt vaguely that something was wrong with their play. It seemed exactly like children playing around any housing development at home, and yet there was something different about it. She looked at Calvin, and saw that he, too, was puzzled.
>
> "Look!" Charles Wallace said suddenly. "They're skipping and bouncing in rhythm! Everyone's doing it at exactly the same moment."
>
> This was so. As the skipping rope hit the pavement, so did the ball. As the rope curved over the head of the jumping child, the child with the ball caught the ball. Down came the ropes. Down came the balls. Over and over again. Up. Down. All in rhythm. All identical. Like the houses. Like the paths. Like the flowers.
>
> Then the doors of all the houses opened simultaneously, and out came women like a row of paper dolls. The print of their dresses was different, but they all gave the appearance of being the same. Each woman stood on the steps of her house. Each clapped. Each child with the ball caught the ball. Each child with the skipping rope folded the rope. Each child turned and walked into the house. The doors clicked shut behind them.

After discussing all the various literary elements encompassed in this short passage (the description of the town, Meg's feelings about the place, Calvin's puzzled looks, the rhythm and repetitiveness of the words in the paragraphs describing the movements of the children and mothers, and finally, the simile), we set off on a drawing lesson on one-point perspective. A perfect opportunity to sketch a scene! Here are the steps to follow:

1. Students should first draw a horizontal line near the top of the paper. This will be the horizon. For this drawing students will need to draw and

erase many of their lines. Make sure you encourage them to press lightly, and to also use a straightedge for accuracy.

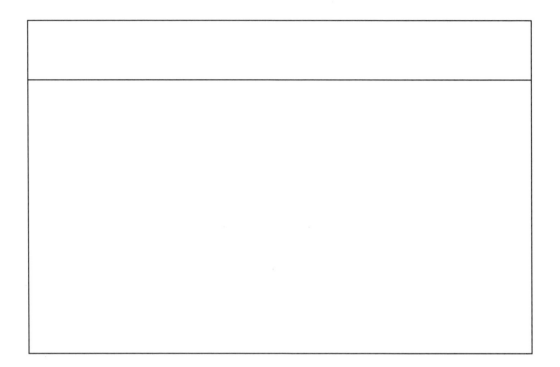

2. Draw a large dot or point in the center of the horizon. This is the vanishing point. All lines will "vanish" into this one point.

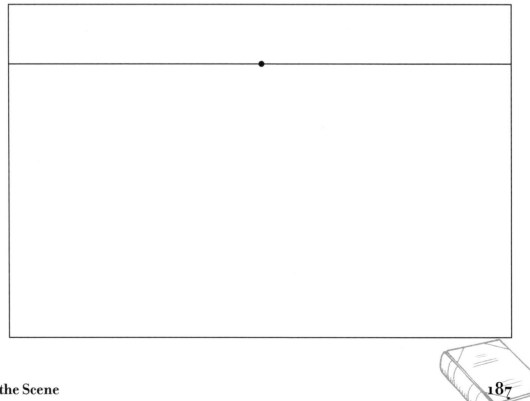

3. Draw two lines that look like an inverted "V" emanating from the vanishing point on the horizon. This will be the road leading through Camazotz.

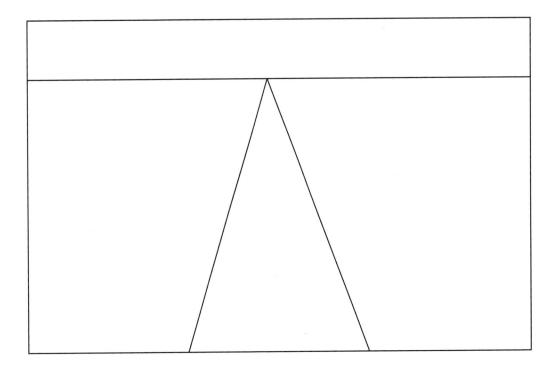

4. Draw two squares, one on each side of the road. Each of these squares will be part of what will eventually become a square house.

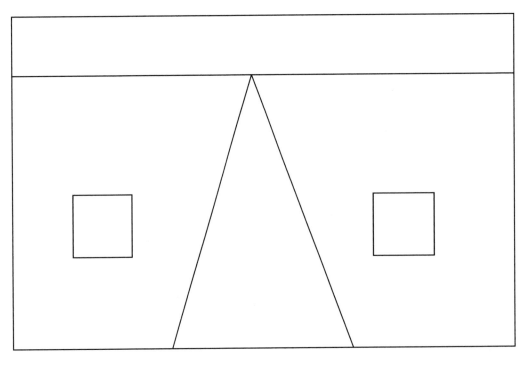

Adventures in Fantasy

5. Draw lines from three corners of each square into the vanishing point on the horizon.

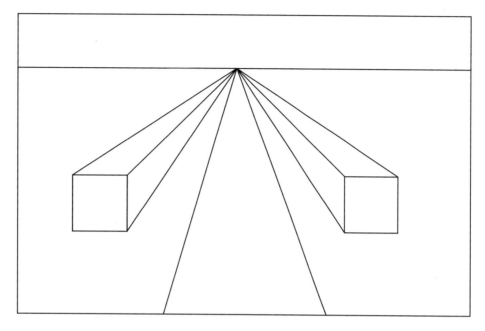

6. Draw horizontal and vertical lines to begin shaping the sides of the houses.

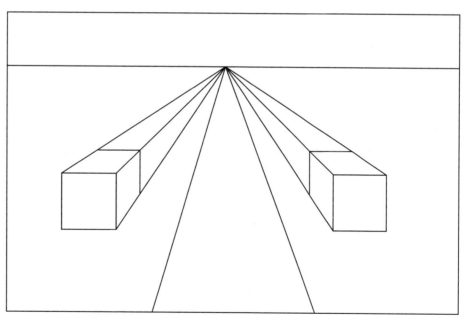

Once everyone has started, students may refer back to *A Wrinkle in Time* and Madeleine L'Engle's description of Camazotz for more detail to guide the drawing.

This is Danna Tan's version of Camazotz. Notice the CENTRAL Intelligence building in the background and "IT" on the pedestal just to the right. Also present are the children skipping rope and bouncing the ball in rhythm at the very same time.

This is Daniel Placenti's one-point perspective drawing of Camazotz. Notice the dark cloud hovering above the CENTRAL Intelligence building in the background.

In the Subterranean City Telos, in *The Temple of Light,* by Mr. Gust

To further warm up students to the idea of sketching their scenes, I like to introduce them to some of J.R.R. Tolkien's artwork. In addition to being a writer, John Ronald Ruel also liked to draw. He was by no means a professional artist, but using colored pencils, ink, and watercolor, he did create quite an abundance of illustrations to accompany his books *The Hobbit* and *The Lord of the Rings* trilogy. Aside from Thror's Map of the lonely mountain, and the map he created of Wilderland, Tolkien also drew illustrations of Mirkwood, The Hill: Hobbiton, The Three Trolls Are Turned to Stone, Rivendell, Beorn's Hall, The Elvenking's Gate, Conversation with Smaug, and my favorite, The Hall at Bag-End, to name just a few. All of these illustrations can be found in the book *J.R.R. Tolkien: Artist and Illustrator,* by Wayne G. Hammond and Christina Scull.

Inspired by Tolkien's example, we student writers then start with our own drawing. Since I consider myself a student of the fine arts of both writing and drawing, I decided to participate in the activity. I went to work sketching a scene for the story I was writing, having no idea how long it would take, or how crude the result would be. Like the writing, it was hard work, yet fun. My students sure did get a kick out of the fact that I was doing it too. And, I believe, they put much greater effort into their own writing and drawing as a result.

I've included the two short excerpts of the writing and the illustration that I shared with my students. In this scene, Taylor Thomas, the heroine of *The Temple of Light,* has passed through a huge portal that has opened on the side of a great, snowcapped mountain. We encounter her walking through a cavern deep inside the bowel of the mountain where the city Telos awaits her discovery:

Taylor had been walking for a good while down the cavern when she rounded a sharp turn. Directly in front of her was a large, gaping opening. For the first time since the dream, here it was: a mystical subterranean city, held deep within the mountain, comfortably concealed under an enormous umbrella-shaped dome. And it was full of life. Huge green leafy plants and tall woody trees of all sorts grew throughout. Colorful birds were flying here and there. Small, gurgling streams flowed lazily into crystal clear pools of water.

Taylor sauntered into the aquarium-like habitat, looking upward in awe at the vastness of the place, spinning round, taking it all in. When she looked closely at the arched ceiling, she realized that she was probably in a large, central atrium of some sort. The sloped roof was striated by a multitude of levels. She could see people walking on balconies, protected from falling into the atrium by a chest-high railing. Within the walls beyond the crowds of people walking on the balconies were various-sized doors. There were also larger openings without doors, exposing different chambers and tunnels that emanated from the atrium outward into the mountain. So mesmerized was Taylor by the sight of the mysterious city, that she didn't even notice that someone had walked up behind her.

"Hello," said a tall, elegant woman with a fine, delicate voice.

Shocked out of her state of enchantment, Taylor turned, stumbled backward and fell first on her buttocks and then onto her back. Raising her head off the hard ground, she looked upward, directly at the long-haired woman. Then, her sight blurred, and she immediately passed out.

Later in the story, after Taylor has spent time healing in this subterranean kingdom with the mysterious woman named Monka, she ventures out again into Telos. Taylor meets Queen Nyla, is joined again by her helper, Zanadar, whom she promptly hugs, and then gazes upon the miraculous wonder of the Temple of Light.

> Loosening her grip around Zanadar's belly, Taylor looked up at his smiling face, then noticed behind him a tall stone tower standing in the center of the atrium. Fascinated by the sight, Taylor moved around Zanadar, to get a better look. The tremendous tower reached from the base of the great room to within a few feet from the top of the domed ceiling. A constant and steady beam of light gushed out the top aperture of the tower, splashed against the ceiling, and poured down the vaulted walls of the atrium, and finally spilled outward into each and every tunnel leading deeper into the mountain. The tower's enormous, cylindrical shaft and cascading waterfall of light captured Taylor's attention. Looking upward, turning round and round, examining her new discovery, Taylor realized for the first time that, aside from the windows that exposed the sun in Monka's home, this tower was the only source of light in the entire city.

Mr. Gust's scene sketch of the subterranean city Telos in his first book of *The Taylor Thomas Trilogy: The Temple of Light*.

"I saw that in my dream," she said finally, while turning back to the queen. "That's where the blast of light came from after the doors of the mountain opened, isn't it?"

Smiling approvingly at Taylor's exuberance, Queen Nyla took two long, graceful strides and stood next to Taylor. "We call it our Temple of Light."

So, if you don't want your students to have all the fun, try developing a story and accompanying illustrations of your own. You'll be amazed at how motivating this can be for your students.

Sketching the Scene Assignment

Get the *Whiteout* Out!

There's a condition in writing called *whiteout*. It's something we definitely want our student writers to avoid. When reading whiteout you can't tell where the characters are anymore! You don't know the location, because it hasn't been identified or described. Everything is white! Use this lesson to help your students realize how important it is to describe the setting, and how much it can help them to sketch the scene first.

Scene Sketch

Use this worksheet to keep your students' scene illustrations in order. When they are finished drawing they can save the illustrations and then cut them out and glue them onto a piece of paper, or scan the images into a computer and paste them into the body of the text.

Scene Summary

Let's say you're reading a really good book with your class and you come across a particular scene that you or your students like, and you decide that you'd like to check your students' comprehension of that scene. Here's a worksheet to assist you in that task. Ask your students to provide a written summary of the scene. You might also want to display an illustration of the scene—if there is one available in the book you're reading—and ask students to write the summary based on the illustration.

Scene Summary Rubric

The rubric provided is designed to assess your students' reading comprehension skills. The summary requires students to summarize and describe the specific events of a scene. Students should be able to identify the main idea (complication, conflict, problem, and so on) of the scene, and to support that summary with a detailed description of the events from the scene. In addition to identifying the conflict of the scene, students should also strive to describe how the conflict was resolved.

Lauren Batucal created this sketch in her story *The Necklace*. In this scene Madicen and Olanna meet the fairy Grace Grateful and three strange birds in the Future Forest.

"You're in Future Forest, I'm Grace Grateful, I'm a Future Forest Fairy." Grace Grateful was actually the shiney purple object that saved the two sisters. Grace Grateful wore purple clothes and also had purple wings. Her face always has a smile on it whenever she flies around Future Forest and whenever she's just doing her job. She has short black smooth hair and eyes that make you want to smile. Grace behaves properly, has manners, and knows well magic.

Adventures in Fantasy

Lizeth Flores created this sketch in her story *The Cruelest Witch*. In this scene Alejandra meets the fairy Butterfly, who is, unfortunately, stuck in a tree. Notice the little yelp of "help" coming from inside the tree.

Jor-El Leos created this sketch in his story *The Amulet Sword*. In this scene the dragon Flames from Pyro Island is stealing the amulet sword so he can "rule the world."

> He jumped into the air and flew over the water pounding his wings as he flew. He was making a screeching sound. When he got to Water Castle all the animals near the castle ran away. He broke the bars and the glass window to the secret room with the Amulet Sword in the stone. He pounded the stone and shattered it! Then he grabbed the sword.

> "I will rule the world!" said Flames in a deep voice. He jumped into the air and flew back to Pyro Island, pounding his

Diego El Jechin created this sketch in his story *The Legend of Amber Amulet*. In this scene Ryan, Henry, and Brian battle the evil Zorardox.

"Why won't you die?" asked Zorardox.

Ryan took his sword and deflected the bolts back. Zorardox was shocked, nearly to death. Then Zorardox used his dark magic to send Henry and Brian flying.

Then Zorardox sent his biggest bolt of lightning, as wide as the cave. Ryan took the blow, and was knocked unconscious. Luckily, Ryan woke up, and with all his might he threw a tremendous bolt at Zorardox. Zorardox was

GET THE WHITEOUT OUT!

The details of a scene must be very precise. Nothing should be left fuzzy or wishy-washy or only partially visualized. There needs to be no doubt that the author has been there, directly in the scene. The more descriptive the author can be, the better readers will feel as though they are part of the scene.

Take a look at the two following scenes. Describe each scene. Which scene do you think you'll be better able to describe? Which description will help readers feel more as though they are part of the scene?

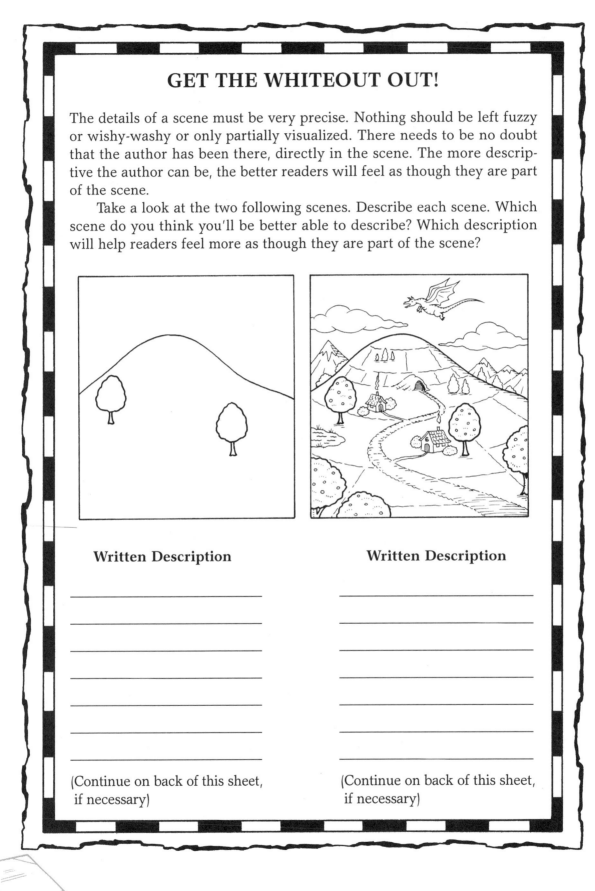

Written Description

_____

_____

_____

_____

_____

_____

(Continue on back of this sheet,
   if necessary)

Written Description

_____

_____

_____

_____

_____

_____

(Continue on back of this sheet,
   if necessary)

SCENE SKETCH

Which scene is this? Circle the correct description.

Exposition   Complication   Conflict #1   Conflict #2   Climax   Resolution

General location: _____

Specific location: _____

Time of day: _____ Season of the year: _____

Weather: _____

Characters involved: _____

_____

_____

SCENE SUMMARY

Book title: _____

Author: _____

Chapter: _____

Which scene is this? Circle the correct description.

Exposition   Complication   Conflict   Climax   Resolution

Other _____

General location: _____

Specific location: _____

Time of day: _____ Season of the year: _____

Weather: _____

Characters involved: _____

_____

_____

Written summary of scene (use extra paper to continue if needed):

_____

_____

_____

_____

_____

_____

_____

_____

_____

SCENE SUMMARY RUBRIC

Goal/ Score	Writing Strategies and Applications
4	• Summary demonstrates well-developed reading comprehension skills and ability to summarize and describe the events of a scene from a story. • Statements that identify and summarize the main idea (the meaning, the point) of the scene are well supported by detailed evidence of specific events from the story. • The written response demonstrates a thorough understanding of a literary work. • Interpretations of text exhibit thoughtful reading.
3	• Summary demonstrates solid reading comprehension skills and ability to summarize and describe the events of a scene from a story. • Statements that identify and summarize the main idea (the meaning, the point) of the scene are supported by detailed evidence of specific events from the story. • The written response demonstrates an adequate understanding of a literary work. • Interpretations exhibit careful reading.
2	• Summary demonstrates some reading comprehension skills and the ability to summarize and describe the events of a scene from a story. • Statements that identify and summarize the main idea (the meaning, the point) of the scene are reported but lack most detailed evidence of specific events from the story. • The written response demonstrates a weak understanding of a literary work. • Interpretations exhibit slipshod, slapdash reading.
1	• Summary demonstrates little or no skill in reading comprehension skills and ability to summarize and describe the events of a scene from a story. • Statements that identify and summarize the main idea (the meaning, the point) of the scene are not fully reported and lack any evidence of specific events from the story. • The written response demonstrates a lack of understanding of a literary work. • Interpretations exhibit careless, thoughtless reading and understanding.

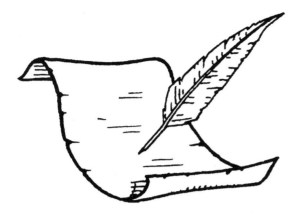

Chapter Nine

Starting the Story

People tend to look at successful writers, writers who are getting their books published and maybe even doing well financially, and think that they sit down at their desks every morning feeling like a million dollars, feeling great about who they are and how much talent they have and what a great story they have to tell; that they take a few deep breaths, push back their sleeves, roll their necks a few times to get all the cricks out, and dive in, typing full formed passages as fast as a court reporter. But this is just the fantasy of the uninitiated.

—Anne Lamott

Invariably, many students have a particularly difficult time getting their stories started. Knowing this, I usually begin the story-starting process with a brief introduction. I tell them to think of this first and rough draft as nothing more than ... *throwing up on the page!* Yes, you read it. That is what I say. And then I pretend to vomit. Right there in front of them at the front of the room. Surprisingly, I've found that this technique actually works. They all get busy writing. Right away! However, I've never been quite sure if they get started to avoid having me do that awful vomit thing again, or if it really does set their minds and hands (and, hopefully, not their stomachs) free. "Just get it down on the page!" I tell them. "Throw up on it! Get those words a-flowing!" I like taunting them.

Can you tell? "Who cares if your words come out wrong! You'll get it right later. The important thing is to get your story started. Don't judge your words and writing. Just write. Right away!"

Yes, I know it sounds rather crude, and quite unorthodox, but that's actually what I say and do. The point here, of course, is that it is important to find some way to get your students writing, to keep them from judging their words even before they get on the page, and to let them know that you, the teacher, are willing to accept just about anything that they direct an honest effort toward.

On their journey, their passage through this "write," the first draft is supposed to be rough. And writers have got to be willing to put themselves—just like the heroes and heroines of their stories—through the muck, the swamps, and maybe even the vomit! Well, thankfully, no student of mine has ever had to wade through any vomit. Their rough drafts have always been much better than that. "So don't worry about it," I tell them. "Your writing won't be as vile as vomit."

With the pressure off to sound perfect the first time, now is the time for students to bring all of the story elements that they have been exploring and working on into one cohesive whole. Their theme, map, travelogue, character descriptions, plot line, scene sketches or illustrations, and various literary elements (that is, alliteration, similes, metaphors, and so on) can all be applied toward the writing of their stories. With these various resources at hand, students can begin the process of cutting and pasting various chunks of prewritten words, sentences, and paragraphs, into the text of their stories. Of course, it won't be that mechanical, but once they begin writing, they'll remember a phrase, or sentence, or description that they have already written, and then they'll go look for it, and eventually, they will weave it into the writing of their story—thus, the reason for all the preliminary writing in the first place. Students are now equipped to begin writing their narratives.

Starting the Story Assignment

On the next several pages you will find a variety of rubrics and reader response pages to choose from. Basically, there are two routes to take. The first route is to break up the evaluation of student narratives into three different parts: beginning, middle, and ending. Because each part requires different elements, it is often more effective to assess each part separately. Doing it this way motivates students to focus more on the elements distinctive to each part. And since a certain amount of detail (setting and character descriptions, dialogue, and so on) may have accumulated because of the preparatory writing already completed, students may write a beginning, middle, or ending that can actually contain five hundred to seven hundred words, or more! Therefore, a separate evaluation for each part is certainly warranted. The second route is to evaluate the entire narrative holistically, as one coherent whole. You will find a rubric and reader response page for evaluating student narratives in this way as well.

Prior to starting the story, or any part of it, it is often helpful to do a quick review of the plot line minilessons in Chapter Six, "Plotting the Path," which discusses the linear path, the Mission in Motion: The Complication, and the circular path. It is important for students to remember what constitutes a *bold beginning, mercurial middle*, and *enticing ending*. And, as always, it is helpful to read, review, and discuss the rubric and reader response page prior to beginning any writing. Students should know what their writing needs to focus on.

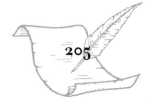

RUBRIC FOR NARRATIVE BEGINNING

Score/ Goal	Writing Strategies and Applications	Writing Conventions
4	• Clearly and consistently uses first- or third-person point of view.	• Writing contains few, if any, errors in spelling, punctuation, capitalization, grammar, and sentence structure.
	• Beginning captures the reader's rapt attention and holds it. Reader is drawn firmly into the story. Exposition and complication are fully developed.	• The errors do not interfere with the reader's understanding of the writing.
	• Characters introduced are lively and realistic (appearance, thoughts, feelings, and actions are clearly described).	
	• Setting is vividly described so the reader can visualize it. Sensory details are used abundantly.	
	• Shows or illustrates the beginning's events. Includes what characters do and say.	
	• Story shows not only revision but also incorporation of reader response comments. Manuscript has been edited and revised to improve the meaning and focus of writing.	
3	• Clearly uses either first- or third-person point of view.	• Writing contains some errors in spelling, punctuation, capitalization, grammar, and sentence structure.
	• Beginning captures the reader's attention. Reader is drawn into the story. Exposition and complication are well developed.	• The errors do not interfere with the reader's understanding of the writing.

Adventures in Fantasy

RUBRIC FOR NARRATIVE BEGINNING
(Continued)

Score/Goal	Writing Strategies and Applications	Writing Conventions
	• Characters introduced are lively and realistic (appearance, thoughts, feelings, and actions are described). • Setting is clearly described. Sensory details are used sufficiently. • Mostly shows rather than tells the beginning's events. • Much or most of the editing and revising of the manuscript has been done to improve the meaning and focus of the writing.	
2	• Uses either a first- or third-person point of view. • Beginning may capture the reader's attention. Reader may be drawn into the story but may not be held there. Either the exposition or complication may not be fully developed. • Characters introduced are overly simplistic. Little attention is given to the appearance, thoughts, feelings, or actions of characters. • Setting is vaguely described. Some sensory details provided. • Mostly tells rather than shows the beginning's events. • Some editing and revising of the manuscript has been completed.	• Writing contains several errors in spelling, punctuation, capitalization, grammar, and sentence structure. • The errors may interfere with the reader's understanding of the writing.

RUBRIC FOR NARRATIVE BEGINNING
(Continued)

Score/ Goal	Writing Strategies and Applications	Writing Conventions
1	• Uses an inconsistent point of view (may switch between first and third person). • Beginning does not capture the reader's attention. Events are merely listed. A complication may not be identified. • Little or no mention of the appearance, thoughts, feelings, or actions of characters. • Setting may or may not be indicated. • Tells rather than shows the beginning's events. • Little or no editing or revising has been completed.	• Writing contains numerous errors in spelling, punctuation, capitalization, grammar, and sentence structure. • The errors interfere with the reader's understanding of the writing.

READER RESPONSE:
NARRATIVE BEGINNING

Readers should keep in mind that the response page should provide the writer with a balance of compliments that encourage and delicately worded suggestions for improvement. For the narrative beginning, readers should write comments that reflect on the following qualities:

- Does the narrative clearly and consistently use either first- or third-person point of view?
- Does the beginning capture the reader's attention and hold it? Is the reader drawn firmly into the story? Are both the exposition (or initial action scene) and complication fully developed?
- Are the characters introduced lively and realistic? Are characters' appearances, thoughts, feelings, and actions clearly described?
- Is the setting vividly described so the reader can visualize it? Are sensory details used abundantly?
- Does the author show or illustrate the beginning's events? Does the author include what characters *do* and *say*?

Name of Reader 1: _____

Comments: _____

_____

_____

_____

_____

_____

Name of Reader 2: _____

Comments: _____

_____

_____

_____

_____

_____

READER RESPONSE:
NARRATIVE BEGINNING
(Continued)

Name of Reader 3: _____

Comments: _____

_____

_____

_____

_____

RUBRIC FOR NARRATIVE MIDDLE

Goal/ Score	Writing Strategies and Applications	Writing Conventions
4	• The point of view remains consistent. • Conflicts are resolved after a significant struggle between the hero and conflict characters. • Conflict characters are lively, realistic, and multidimensional. Appearance, actions, strengths, weaknesses are clearly described. • New settings are vividly described so the reader can visualize it. Sensory details are used abundantly. • Each event clearly shows what characters do and say. • Shows not only revision but also incorporation of reader response comments. Manuscript has been thoroughly edited and revised to improve the meaning and focus of writing.	• Writing contains few, if any, errors in spelling, punctuation, capitalization, grammar, and sentence structure. • The errors do not interfere with the reader's understanding of the writing.
3	• The point of view remains consistent. • Conflicts are resolved after a struggle between the hero and conflict characters or obstacles. • Conflict characters are realistic and multidimensional. Appearance, actions, strengths, and weaknesses are described.	• Writing contains some errors in spelling, punctuation, capitalization, grammar, and sentence structure. • The errors do not interfere with the reader's understanding of the writing.

RUBRIC FOR NARRATIVE MIDDLE
(Continued)

Goal/ Score	Writing Strategies and Applications	Writing Conventions
	• New settings are clearly described. Sensory details are used sufficiently. • Each event mostly shows what characters do and say. • Much or most of the editing and revising of the manuscript has been done to improve the meaning and focus of the writing.	
2	• The point of view remains consistent but may switch from third-person limited to third-person omnipotent. • Conflicts are resolved, but only after a minor or insignificant struggle with the conflict characters or obstacles. • Conflict characters are overly simplistic. Little attention is given to their appearance, actions, strengths, and weaknesses. • Settings are vaguely described. Some sensory details are provided. • Mostly tells or lists rather than shows or illustrates the events. • Some editing and revising of the manuscript has been completed.	• Writing contains several errors in spelling, punctuation, capitalization, grammar, and sentence structure. • The errors may interfere with the reader's under-standing of the writing.

RUBRIC FOR NARRATIVE MIDDLE
(Continued)

Goal/ Score	Writing Strategies and Applications	Writing Conventions
1	• The narrative uses an inconsistent point of view (may switch between first and third person). • Conflicts are resolved with little or no apparent struggle with conflict characters or obstacles. Events are merely listed. • Little or no mention of the appearance and actions, thoughts and feelings, strengths and weaknesses of characters. • Settings may or may not be indicated. • Tells rather than shows the middle's events. • Little or no editing or revising has been completed.	• Writing contains numerous errors in spelling, punctuation, capitalization, grammar, and sentence structure. • The errors interfere with the reader's understanding of the writing.

READER RESPONSE: NARRATIVE MIDDLE

Readers should keep in mind that the response page should provide the writer with a balance of compliments that encourage and delicately worded suggestions for improvement. For the narrative middle, readers should write comments that reflect upon the following qualities:

- Does the author's point of view remain consistent?
- Does the author resolve each conflict only after a significant struggle between the hero and conflict characters or obstacles? Is each conflict accompanied with a thrust downward in the hero's predicament and then a counterthrust upward as the hero barely resolves the conflict?
- Are the new conflict characters introduced lively, realistic, and multidimensional? Are the characters' appearances and actions clearly described?
- Are all new settings vividly described so the reader can visualize them? Are sensory details used abundantly?
- Do all new events show what characters *do* and *say*?

Name of Reader 1: _____

Comments: _____

_____

_____

_____

_____

_____

Name of Reader 2: _____

Comments: _____

_____

_____

_____

_____

_____

Adventures in Fantasy

READER RESPONSE: NARRATIVE MIDDLE
(Continued)

Name of Reader 3: _____

Comments: _____

_____

_____

_____

_____

RUBRIC FOR NARRATIVE ENDING

Goal/ Score	Writing Strategies and Applications	Writing Conventions
4	• Point of view has remained consistent. • Climax is the most exciting and tension-filled scene in the story. Complication is fully resolved. • Additional characters introduced are lively, realistic, and multidimensional. Their appearances and actions, thoughts and feelings, strengths and weaknesses are clearly described. • Villain's domain is vividly described so the reader can visualize it. Sensory details are used abundantly. • Shows or illustrates the ending's events. Includes what characters do and say. • Story shows not only revision but also incorporation of reader response comments. Manuscript has been edited and revised to improve the meaning and focus of writing.	• Writing contains few, if any, errors in spelling, punctuation, capitalization, grammar, and sentence structure. • The errors do not interfere with the reader's understanding of the writing.

RUBRIC FOR NARRATIVE ENDING
(Continued)

Goal/ Score	Writing Strategies and Applications	Writing Conventions
3	• Point of view has remained consistent. • Climax is an exciting and tension-filled scene. Complication is resolved. • Additional characters introduced are realistic and multidimensional. Appearances and actions, thoughts and feelings, strengths and weaknesses are sufficiently described. • Villain's domain is clearly described so the reader can visualize it. Sensory details are used sufficiently. • Mostly shows rather than tells the ending's events. • Much or most of the editing and revising of the manuscript has been done to improve the meaning and focus of the writing.	• Writing contains some errors in spelling, punctuation, capitalization, grammar, and sentence structure. • The errors do not interfere with the reader's understanding of the writing.
2	• Uses either a first- or third-person point of view. • Climax may capture the reader's attention. Complication may not be resolved. • Characters introduced are overly simplistic. Little attention is given to their	• Writing contains several errors in spelling, punctuation, capitalization, grammar, and sentence structure. • The errors may interfere with the reader's understanding of the writing.

RUBRIC FOR NARRATIVE ENDING
(Continued)

Goal/ Score	Writing Strategies and Applications	Writing Conventions
	appearance, action, thoughts, feelings, strengths, and weaknesses. • Setting is vaguely described. Some sensory details provided. • Mostly tells rather than shows the ending's events. • Some editing/revising of the manuscript has been completed.	
1	• Uses an inconsistent point of view (may switch between first and third person). • Climax does not capture the reader's attention. Events are merely listed. A resolution may not be identified. • Little or no mention of the appearance, thoughts, feelings, or actions of characters. • Setting may or may not be indicated. • Tells rather than shows the ending's events. • Little or no editing or revising has been completed.	• Writing contains numerous errors in spelling, punctuation, capitalization, grammar, and sentence structure. • The errors interfere with the reader's understanding of the writing.

READER RESPONSE: NARRATIVE ENDING

Readers should keep in mind that the response page should provide the writer with a balance of compliments that encourage and delicately worded suggestions for improvement. For the narrative ending, readers should write comments that reflect on the following qualities:

- Has the point of view remained consistent?
- Is the climax the most exciting and tension-filled scene in the story? Has the complication been resolved? Has the hero returned home for the final resolution?
- Are additional characters introduced lively, realistic, and multi-dimensional? Have their appearances, actions, thoughts, feelings, strengths, and weaknesses been clearly described?
- Has the villain's domain been vividly described so the reader can visualize it? Have sensory details been used abundantly?
- Does the author show or illustrate the ending's events? Has the author included what characters *do* and *say*?

Name of Reader 1: _____

Comments: _____

_____

_____

_____

_____

Name of Reader 2: _____

Comments: _____

_____

_____

_____

_____

READER RESPONSE: NARRATIVE ENDING
(Continued)

Name of Reader 3: _____

Comments: _____

_____

_____

_____

_____

_____

_____

RUBRIC FOR NARRATIVE

Goal/ Score	Writing Strategies and Applications	Writing Conventions
4	• Narrative consistently uses first- or third-person point of view. • Plot line clearly describes the course of action (exposition, complication, conflicts, climax, and resolution). • Characters are lively and realistic. Appearance, thoughts, feelings, and actions are clearly described. • Setting is vividly described. Sensory details are plentiful. • Shows or illustrates the events of the story. Includes what characters do and say. • Story shows not only revision but also incorporation of reader response comments. Story has been edited and revised to improve the meaning and focus of the writing. • The theme is vividly clear without being stated.	• Writing contains few, if any, errors in spelling, punctuation, capitalization, grammar, and sentence structure. • The errors do not interfere with the reader's understanding of the writing.
3	• Narrative clearly uses either first- or third-person point of view. • Plot line adequately describes the course of action (exposition, complication, conflicts, climax, and resolution).	• Writing contains some errors in spelling, punctuation, capitalization, grammar, and sentence structure. • The errors do not interfere with the reader's understanding of the writing.

RUBRIC FOR NARRATIVE
(Continued)

Goal/ Score	Writing Strategies and Applications	Writing Conventions
	• Characters are realistic. Appearance, thoughts, feelings, and actions are described. • Setting is clearly described. Sensory details are used. • Shows rather than tells the events of the story. • Much or most of the editing and revising has been done to improve the meaning and focus of the writing. • The theme is clear but may also be explained unnecessarily.	
2	• Narrative uses either a first- or third-person point of view. • Events of the story are listed with little attention to detail. Complication is vaguely mentioned. Narrative may not have a clear ending (climax and resolution). • Little attention is given to the appearance, thoughts, feelings, or actions of characters. • Setting is vaguely described. Some sensory details provided. • Mostly tells rather than shows the events of story.	• Writing contains several errors in spelling, punctuation, capitalization, grammar, and sentence structure. • The errors may interfere with the reader's understanding of the writing.

RUBRIC FOR NARRATIVE
(Continued)

Goal/Score	Writing Strategies and Applications	Writing Conventions
	• Some editing and revising have been completed.	
	• The theme is hazy and uncertain.	
1	• Narrative uses an inconsistent point of view (may switch between first and third person).	• Writing contains numerous errors in spelling, punctuation, capitalization, grammar, and sentence structure.
	• Plot line is not developed and ideas are merely listed. A complication may not be identified and the story may end abruptly (lacking a climax and resolution).	• The errors interfere with the reader's understanding of the writing.
	• Little or no mention of the appearance, thoughts, feelings, or actions of characters.	
	• Setting may or may not be indicated.	
	• Little or no editing or revising have been done to the manuscript to improve the meaning and focus of the writing.	
	• The theme is unclear or nonexistent.	

READER RESPONSE: NARRATIVE

Readers should keep in mind that the response page should provide the writer with a balance of compliments that encourage and delicately worded suggestions for improvement. For the narrative, readers should write comments that reflect on the following qualities:

- Does the narrative clearly and consistently use either first- or third-person point of view?
- Does the plot line clearly describe the course of action (exposition, complication, conflicts, climax, and resolution)?
- Are the characters lively, realistic, and multidimensional? Have their appearances, actions, thoughts, feelings, strengths, and weaknesses been clearly described?
- Have the various settings been vividly described so the reader can visualize them? Are sensory details used abundantly?
- Are the events of the story shown or illustrated? Does the author include what characters *do* and *say*?
- Is the theme vividly clear without being stated?

Name of Reader 1: _____

Comments: _____

_____

_____

_____

_____

_____

Name of Reader 2: _____

Comments: _____

_____

_____

_____

_____

_____

Adventures in Fantasy

READER RESPONSE: NARRATIVE
(Continued)

Name of Reader 3: _____

Comments: _____

_____

_____

_____

_____

Chapter Ten

Trimming the Tale

I write, reread, and rewrite with a revision consciousness. That is, I value revision, strive to revise where and when doing so makes sense, and take responsibility for revision because I care about the reading. We want students to do the same and to write and revise with a mindset of will my writing make sense to my readers? Will it engage them?

—Regie Routman

As we approach the end of our adventure in fantasy writing we can now focus on the process of trimming the tale. This is the fix-it-up/clean-it-up stage of writing where both revision and editing/proofreading occur. During this stage, students have their rough drafts read by a few peer readers; acquire some carefully worded suggestions about how to improve their work; revisit and reflect upon their writing; and then revise the piece, confer with the teacher, and then write the final copy of their story. Let's take a look at how the whole process works.

Writers' Workshop

During writers' workshop, some students will be found working on a rough draft, others will be reading another student's rough draft and responding to that writing, others will be working on a revision of a part of their story, others will be conferring with the teacher, some will be working on a scene illustration, and still others will be working on a final copy. During writers' workshop the classroom is a very busy place. Some students will be gathered under a map hanging on the wall, asking questions, pointing, laughing. Some will be lying on their bellies on the floor, silently writing away. Others will be in a small group, busy talking about their classmate's story, explaining their written responses.

For me, when a writers' workshop is working like this, it's as though the workshop with all its student writer heroes and sidekicks have taken off on a grand adventure, and everyone is in the heart of the journey, the nadir, the supreme ordeal, the highest point of glory, the greatest moment of triumph. Everyone is writing, conferring with each other, steering their stories, trimming their tales. It's a wonderful experience, and knowing that you had something to do with it happening makes it all the more worthwhile.

To make this kind of writers' workshop experience happen, you must set up the classroom in advance so that everybody is aware of all the procedures, processes, locations of materials, and codes of behavior. Generally, it's best to start each workshop with a quick review of what's going on. I find it helpful to invite students to write their names on the board according to specific categories that I need identified. This way each person's job is in clear view and everybody knows who is doing what. The categories change all the time, according to the needs of the workshop. And students erase and then rewrite their names in another category, as needed, as well. Here is an example of some typical categories:

- Ready to Read a Rough Draft
- Working on a Revision of _____
- Working on a Rough Draft of _____
- Working on a Final Copy of _____
- Waiting for a Reader
- Waiting for a Conference with Mr. Gust

It is very helpful to have a plentiful supply of readers at the ready, eager to respond. Generally speaking, readers are those people who have finished a rough draft of a particular piece of writing as assigned (beginning, middle, or end) and are on, or ahead of, schedule. To do this most effectively, try to have everyone's rough draft finished at the same time. That way, everyone is both ready to read and waiting for a reader.

Readers Respond

When all the hero and heroine student writers begin to read and respond to each other's writing, they need to know that the goal is for them all to gradually gain a certain level of sophistication in being able to help another writer look at his or her own writing from a different point of view. To respond effectively, one must help the writer look again at a piece of writing, not with the same

eyes but from a new perspective. Likewise, the author, in order to revise, must "re-see" a piece of writing in a whole new light. Revising requires reflection and the recognition that another way to write a piece is possible. Writers must also be sophisticated enough to recognize a gap between what their intentions were and what another reader actually reads on the page.

At first, I tend to allow students an opportunity to pick those whom they want to read their story. These "friends" are the people they can trust. After all, they're exposing their own growing creation, and it's therefore wise at first to choose an eager reader over one who doesn't have much interest. This usually gets students loosened up and used to the idea of letting someone else read their writing.

Before beginning, readers should be taught how to respond. Good readers know that they must first offer some encouragement, and then provide a few gently worded suggestions for improvement. It should also be taught that these suggestions be written in the form of a question. For example: "Do you think it would help to describe your settings with a little more detail? What does the Enchanted Forest look like?" Or, "Do you think it would help build more tension in your story if the conflict wasn't resolved so quickly?" Or, "What was this character thinking or feeling when she entered the villain's domain?"

Next, after at least three readers have written a response to a writer's work, the writers can go back to their writing, look over the written responses, and then reflect back on their work while keeping in mind the suggestions the other readers have provided. This is when writers should be thinking about what they might do to improve their work. Then, after a period of reflection and "re-seeing," they can dig back into the piece and begin to revise the work. To do all of this, if you are to have a true reflective writing classroom, you will have to give your students plenty of time. This means that your students may need to write at least four days out of five. If too many days go by without your students having the chance to continue writing, they will most likely lose touch with their thinking and may have to spend a good part of a writing session reorienting themselves to their story and their original intentions.

Conferencing and Connecting with Students

Once students have written their rough draft, had at least three different readers respond to their writing, and completed the entire rewrite of the piece, I then sit down with them for a conference. Typically, I don't confer with students unless they've had at least three readers respond to their writing and they have completed a revision of their work. I sometimes tell my students, "You don't expect me to read something the first time you write it, do you?" I know that sounds a little harsh, and at times I do confer with students when they're writing their rough drafts or going through a revision, but to be honest, I like to pretend that I'm some kind of masterful wizard and I don't bother myself with the words of the uninitiated. I try to make them feel as though it's a privilege to have me read their writing. I find that with the powerful wizard persona firmly in place, it helps to create a little fun, and sense of challenge as well.

I also like to tell students about how in a literary agent's office, or even an editor's office at a big-time publisher, they have what are called *first readers*. First readers are the gatekeepers to the throne. Agents and editors don't read just any old manuscript. They are the "kings" in their office. And before the kings read anyone's writing, the writing has to first make it past the gatekeepers. The gatekeepers in our class, of course, are the peer readers who respond to the writing in the first place.

When conferencing with students I like to keep in mind a scene in *The Hobbit* where Gandalf and the dwarfs are seated around the table in Bilbo's home, examining Thror's map. Thror was Thorin's grandfather, you know, and Thorin is the head dwarf of the unlucky band of thirteen. Gandalf unfolds the map, spreads it out on the table, and asks Bilbo to bring over a lamp. Bilbo, who loves maps, approaches the table, carrying with him a lamp and a keen sense of awe and wonder. I try to be like Bilbo and bring along that same love of maps and good stories when I go conferring with students. If I had a little red lamp, to perhaps shed a little light on their map and story, I'd take that along, too.

Other times, depending on the writer's ability to comprehend my sense of humor, I ask students to come to me, at the conference table, while I'm sitting there with their map and writing. Sometimes, they have to come shed a little light on what I view as huge holes in their stories. I like to pretend I'm Gandalf, the one orchestrating the entire affair, perhaps even holding their lives in my very hands. I give them a nasty scowl looking as if I'm about to send them on another perilous journey of yet another rewrite. Students know I'm kidding, because they really do get a sense that I love reading their stories. And I do. And that's the key. If students know that you enjoy reading their stories, no matter how bad their writing may be, then they are going to enjoy having you read, review, and discuss their work. It's really that simple. If they can see and hear you laughing, having fun with another student, going over that kid's story, struggling with her to really make sense of it, taking a keen interest in her progress as a writer, then everyone else in the class will look forward to the time when you, the teacher, are scheduled to review their writing.

At times I find it necessary to confer with both the writer and the three readers who have all written comments on the writer's reader response page. When I do this, it is usually because one or all of the readers have failed to comment on something that is glaringly wrong with the writer's work. For instance, if a student's story is totally devoid of any description of a new character when that character is introduced in a scene, or no description is provided of a new setting encountered on the hero's journey, I find it necessary to have a meeting of the minds. When these things happen—and they often do—I feel it is important to go over my response to the writing and ask the readers why they didn't write comments pertaining to these issues. I do this for a number of reasons. First, I need to determine if all the students involved have simply missed these important points. If so, the conference serves as an opportunity to reteach a concept that was introduced originally during a minilesson that the students appeared to have missed. Second, I need to determine if the readers who were responding didn't take the time or spend the effort to write comments pertaining to the issues at hand. If so, it is sometimes because the readers were friends of the writer and didn't want to offend the writer. When this happens I try to explain that writers depend on the readers to help them become aware of anything they may have missed, and that the writers' grade or score for the writing is actually dependent on their help. I try to explain to everyone sitting at the conference table that we are all in this together, and that these problems should have been taken care of before I received the revised version of the piece. So, I tell them, if you really want to be a good friend, you'll take the time to look for any weaknesses in your friend's writing, and you'll have the courage to be honest with your friend and tell the truth.

Revising

The Mechanics of Revision

Most students, if you ask them, don't have a clue as to what really happens during the revision stage of writing. They don't know the mechanics involved in the revision process. After students have all written their rough drafts and are ready and waiting to read and comment on each other's writing, I first introduce them to the various mechanisms of revision. To do this, start out first with the worksheet provided here. Go over all the various types of revisions with your students to prepare them for the revision process. Once the revising starts, it's a good idea to review your students' efforts. When you find specific examples of the various forms of revision, make overhead copies of the effective revision techniques (adding, inserting, changing, repairing, clarifying, rearranging, shifting, erasing, deleting, or consolidating), and provide a short minilesson that highlights those students' efforts.

Proofreading

In addition to all the revising that you and your students will be doing during this trimming-of-the-tale phase of the writing process, you'll want to make certain that your students are aware of the various proofreading symbols that will find their way onto their papers. Personally, I find separating the two steps in the writing process—revising and editing/proofreading—to be counterproductive. I see no reason why students can't be doing some proofreading while also revising. Surely, during the first rewrite of the rough draft, you'll want your students to focus more on revising their work, but if a few simple errors are detected and can be easily fixed, then why not? Of course, after all the revising has been completed, then you'll want your students focusing primarily on proofreading prior to writing their final copies.

THE MECHANICS OF REVISION

Now is the time to begin trimming your tale, which means that you'll be revising your rough draft. If you are going to revise your writing, you'll need to "re-see" your work from another perspective. Once you take a new look and decide that your writing could use some changes, you'll need to know the "mechanical" options you have available to make these changes. Let's take a look at the various ways you can trim your tale.

ADDING AND INSERTING

The first way to revise your writing is to add some information; this happens when you discover that this kind of information is missing. You don't have to add this new information to the end of your work, you know. It is possible to add and insert the new information right into the story in its natural order, where you think it belongs. So wherever the information is needed, simply add it right there!

CHANGING, REPAIRING, AND CLARIFYING

Let's say you reread one of the sentences you wrote and decide that it just really doesn't quite sound right or make sense. What are you going to do? Well, when changing, repairing, or clarifying your writing, sometimes you'll need to shorten or lengthen a sentence, or rearrange some of the words in that sentence. Maybe what you wrote was a sentence fragment or a run-on. Now you'll need to go back and rework the words or sentence to make it sound better.

REARRANGING AND SHIFTING (CUT AND PASTE)

What happens if you decide that you wrote an entire paragraph in entirely the wrong place? Did you know that you can actually move an entire paragraph if it needs to be in a new, better location? You can! Just rearrange the whole page if you need to! Move those paragraphs where they really need to go.

ERASING, DELETING, AND CONSOLIDATING

Now, let's say that you want every word in every sentence, paragraph, or scene to be just right. Would something sound better if it were shorter? Do you need to eliminate unnecessary adverbs? Have you repeated certain descriptions or events unnecessarily? When erasing, deleting, and consolidating, you are doing a "clean-it-up" or "fix-it-up" kind of revision. Writers who trim their tales in this way are interested in making certain that everything sounds just right.

PROOFREADING

This table shows standard proofreading marks, which you may find helpful to use.

Editor's Mark	Meaning
	Delete
	Capitalize
	Use lowercase
	Insert or add a word
	Spelling error
	Reverse letters or words (transpose)
	Add a period
	Add a comma
	Add an apostrophe
	Add quotation marks
	Begin a new paragraph (indent)
	Make a space
	Close the space

Trimming the Tale

Chapter Eleven

Booking the Boon

The book is what is real. You read it, you and it form a relationship, perhaps a trivial one, perhaps a deep and lasting one. As you read it word by word and page by page, you participate in its creation, just as a cellist playing a Bach suite participates, note by note, in the creation, the coming-to-be, the existence, of the music. And, as you read and reread, the book, of course, participates in the creation of you, your thoughts and feelings, the size and temper of your soul.

—Ursula K. Le Guin

So, what is the reward—the boon—that your student writer heroes will receive now that their perilous journey—their adventure in fantasy—is complete? Well … their very own book, of course! To acquire the boon, one must book it in advance. You must engage your students prior to beginning, by letting them know that there will be a great and glorious treasure at the end of their journey. It's called the boon. The reward. So, book your students for their boon. Call it a contract, if you like, for your students to perform at a specified time, but this "booking of the boon" is a demonstration of the high expectations that you as the teacher must have in order for your students to complete this most difficult of projects.

Publishing and bookbinding can be as simple as stapling a story between two sheets of construction paper. However, if your students have put in the time and effort to write a complete and cohesive fantasy story, you may want to facilitate a special workshop that will do their stories justice. Here is how to get started.

Booking the Boon Workshop

To begin this bookmaking workshop it is a good idea to start with a thorough examination of books that have already been published. I like to pass out a plethora of fantasy books so that students can explore the front and back covers, title page, acknowledgments and dedications, tables of contents, and author pages so that they can see for themselves what items go into the making and publishing of a book. The most challenging page to write by far is definitely the back cover, where the story teaser is located. To help students write an effective teaser my classes take a good look at as many back covers as possible. This helps students become familiar with how much information about the story to disclose in the teaser and what to leave out in order to whet readers' appetites for reading the book. We also discuss what story teasers are the most effective and why. When you're finished reviewing the books, pass out the Booking the Boon Workshop worksheets and read through the explanations, paying special attention to the back cover and story teaser, and then have your students get started.

Bookmaking

With the six additional book pages complete, now is the time to bind all the story's pages together. Since the front and back covers have already been completed, binding the book could be as simple as slipping the entire manuscript into a presentation folder that has clear, see-through front and back pages. This will allow your students' illustrations for the front cover, and text for the back cover, to be properly displayed. If you want to go all-out, you could facilitate a bookbinding session that creates hinged, cloth-covered covers.

To do this, you'll need a few materials:

- scissors

- ruler

- glue

- tagboard, cardboard, or poster board

- cloth book tape

- wallpaper, cloth, wrapping paper, contact paper, or paper grocery bag

- heaveyweight construction paper or poster board

- drill or hammer and nail

- string, shoelaces, ribbon, or yarn

Bookmaking Instructions

1. Cut two 9- by 12-inch pieces of tagboard, cardboard, or poster board.

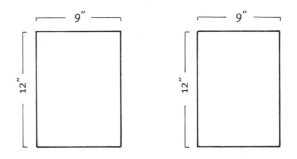

2. Cut a 1-inch strip from both the front and back covers. Then using the cloth book tape, tape the strips together on the inside, leaving an ⅛-inch space open between the two strips.

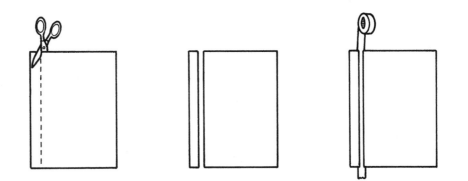

3. If you wish to display the title, illustration, and back cover text that your students have already written, you will need to cut out an appropriately sized window from both covers.

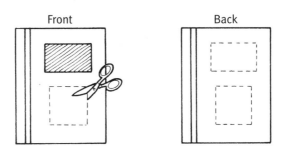

Front   Back

4. Next, cut two pieces of wallpaper, cloth, wrapping paper, contact paper, or a paper grocery bag that is approximately ¾-inch wider (both top to bottom and side to side) than the tagboard, cardboard, or poster board. Then cut out the appropriate amount of this material to accommodate

the windows that have also already been cut from the front and back covers. Make sure you also leave ¾-inch of material so that it can be folded through the window to cover the tagboard, cardboard, or poster board.

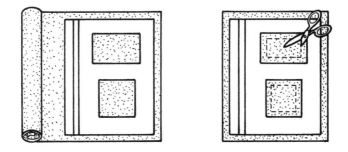

5. Place the tagboard, cardboard, or poster board on the cover material; miter the corners; cut diagonal slits in the excess cover material for the windows; fold in all the edges; and glue.

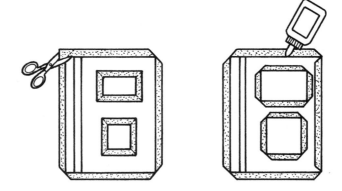

6. Then place the front and back cover illustrations and text onto the covered tagboard, cardboard, or poster board. Make sure the illustrations and text are fully exposed in the windows. Then cut two additional pieces of heavyweight paper or poster board that are approximately 7 by 11 inches and place them on the inside of the front and back covers. (These will provide support to prevent the front and back cover illustrations and text from being torn.) Then glue the pieces into place. Now the front and back covers are complete.

Back of front cover

Adventures in Fantasy

7. Place the entire manuscript, complete with illustrations, cover page, acknowledgments and dedication page, table of contents page, and about the author page, between the two covers. Then punch at least three holes into the one-inch strips. You can do this by using a drill or hammer and nail.

8. Finally, lace the string, shoelaces, ribbon, or yarn through the holes and tie together. The book is now complete!

With your students' books complete, now is the time for you and your students to celebrate. Don't forget: whether it's simply with the heroic student writers in your classroom or with family and friends in attendance too, you and your students should share your feelings of accomplishment with plenty of ceremony. Make certain you give your students the opportunity to give thanks to all those who have participated in the journey.

BOOKING THE BOON WORKSHOP

Now that your story is complete, you're done, right? Wrong! You've got a story and illustrations, but you don't have the boon, or the reward, yet, do you? So what's the boon, the reward for all your efforts? Well ... a book, of course! All you have now is an unbound pile of papers. That's a story, but not a book! To turn your story into a full-fledged book, you'll need to complete a few more tasks.

FRONT COVER

First and foremost, your story is going to need a title. Of course, the title will be central to your book's front cover. Second, you will need to put your name—the author's name—on the cover as well. Don't bother to write "written by" or "by" before your name, because everyone knows by now that the name on the front cover of any book is the author of the story. Finally, you'll probably want to draw an illustration for the cover. The illustration should somehow capture the essence of the story. You could draw an illustration of a particular place, or scene in the story, or an important character such as the hero or heroine, or ... you decide!

COVER PAGE

The cover page should be the first page readers encounter when they first open the front cover. The cover page should be a simple page with the printed words of the title, the author, and the publisher included. As for the "publisher" of your book, you could use the school's name, or simply make up a name of a make-believe company for fun.

DEDICATION AND ACKNOWLEDGMENTS PAGE

A dedication is a short piece of text at the beginning of a written work that associates it with somebody esteemed by the author. Decide whom you'd like to dedicate all your hard work to. It could be one or several of your friends, someone in your family, or even your teacher.

An acknowledgment is an expression of thanks or appreciation. You'll need to decide whom you would like to thank for helping you write your story. Did your family, your classmates, a friend, or your teacher help you?

TABLE OF CONTENTS

The table of contents is a simple listing of the chapters and the page numbers on which they begin. You may also want to provide a list of illustrations or maps that are included in your book.

ABOUT THE AUTHOR PAGE

Now that all the front pages of your book are done, we turn to the back of the book. The very last page of your book should include a description of you, the author. This "About the Author" page should be written from a third-person point of view. It should sound as though someone else has written it about you. You'll probably want to include some personal information about yourself, like your hobbies, what you do for fun, what grade you're in, your experience as a writer, where you live, and so on. You decide.

BACK COVER

The back cover of your book needs to have two basic parts: the story teaser or summary, and several complimentary quotes from reviewers.

The story teaser or summary is often difficult to write. It's called a *teaser* because its job is to entice someone who happens to pick up the book into wanting to read it. It should "tease" the potential reader into opening the front cover and digging into the story. Your story teaser should be long enough to give a basic plot summary that reveals the who, the what, the when, the where, the how, and the why of your story, but it shouldn't be so long that it gives away the exciting ending. Remember, you want to motivate people to read your story so they can find out what happens at the end.

Here are some basic issues your story teaser should address:

- What does your hero or heroine dream for, long for, wish for, need?
- What is the problem he or she desperately needs to solve?
- What is the personal fear or weakness that your hero or heroine must overcome?
- What steps must your hero or heroine take to realize his or her dream, overcome his or her fear, or solve his or her problem?
- What is at stake in your story? Mention the page-turning tension and the deadline or ticking clock that your hero or heroine will need to meet or beat in order to save their endangered world.

After you have completed your story teaser, you will next want to include a few complimentary quotes by some "expert" reviewers. These so-called experts could be fellow classmates who have read some or all of your story. Pick a few quotes that were written on the reader response pages that accompanied the rubrics for your story. And maybe a family member has been reading your story all along. What do these "experts" have to say about your story? And what did your teacher have to say about your writing? Surely some of them provided a compliment or two that you could use!

Bibliography

Bassham, G., and Bronson, E. (eds.). *The Lord of the Rings and Philosophy: One Book to Rule Them All.* Chicago: Open Court, 2003.

Brooks, T., and others. *The Writer's Complete Fantasy Reference.* Cincinnati: Writer's Digest Books, 1998.

Campbell, J. *The Hero with a Thousand Faces.* Princeton, N.J.: Princeton University Press, 1968.

Card, O. S. *How to Write Science Fiction & Fantasy.* Cincinnati: Writer's Digest Books, 1990.

Farmer, N. *The House of the Scorpion.* New York: Simon Pulse, 2002.

Hammond, W. G., and Scull, C. *J.R.R. Tolkien: Artist and Illustrator.* Boston: Houghton Mifflin, 1995.

Keen, S., and Valley-Fox, A. *Your Mythic Journey: Finding Meaning in Your Life Through Writing and Storytelling.* New York: Putnam, 1973.

Kilian, C. *Writing Science Fiction and Fantasy.* Bellingham, Wash.: Self-Counsel Press, 1998.

Lamott, A. *Bird by Bird: Some Instructions on Writing and Life.* New York: Anchor Books, 1994.

Le Guin, Ursula K. *The Language of the Night: Essays on Fantasy and Science Fiction.* New York: HarperCollins, 1989. (Originally published 1979.)

L'Engle, M. *A Wrinkle in Time.* New York: Dell, 1962.

Martin, P. (ed.). *The Writer's Guide to Fantasy Literature: From Dragon's Lair to Hero's Quest.* Waukesha, Wis.: Writer Books, 2002.

Murphy, R. *Imaginary Worlds: Notes on a New Curriculum.* New York: Teachers and Writers Collaborative, 1974.

Ochoa, G., and Osier, J. *The Writer's Guide to Creating a Science Fiction Universe.* Cincinnati: Writer's Digest Books, 1993.

Page, M., and Ingpen, R. *Encyclopedia of Things That Never Were: Creatures, Places, and People.* New York: Penguin Books, 1985.

Paolini, C. *Eragon.* New York: Knopf, 2003.

Rodari, G. *The Grammar of Fantasy: An Introduction to the Art of Inventing Stories.* New York: Teachers and Writers Collaborative, 1996.

Routman, R. *Writing Essentials: Raising Expectations and Results While Simplifying Teaching.* Portsmouth, N.H.: Heinemann, 2005.

Rozelle, R. *Description and Setting: Techniques and Exercises for Crafting a Believable World of People, Places and Events.* Cincinnati: Writer's Digest Books, 2005.

Tolkien, J.R.R. *Tree and Leaf.* New York: HarperCollins, 2001. (Originally published 1964.)

Yolen, J. *Touch Magic: Fantasy, Faerie & Folklore in the Literature of Childhood.* Little Rock, Ark.: August House, 1981.

Index

Whiteout, 193; Get the Whiteout Out!
  worksheet, 198
Wizards, 14, 97
Words, 14; dialogue, 152–153; figurative language,
  154–156; sensory, 47, 55–56; sounds of, 156–158;
  transition, 60
World building, 30
Wrinkle in Time, A (L'Engle), 2, 186–189
Writers' workshop, 227–228
Writing prompt, 45–46

Y

Yolen, Jane, 23, 151
Young adult fantasy, popularity of, 7
Young, Cheyenne, 129

Z

Ziggurats, 24

Other Books of Interest

Writing for a Change

Boosting Literacy and Learning Through Social Action

National Writing Project

Paper	ISBN: 978-0-7879-8657-5
	www.josseybass.com

"This is the book educators have been waiting for: practitioner guidance on combining literacy education and community problem solving to create a powerful form of service-learning in which students can master critical academic and civic competencies."
> —**Betsey McGee, former senior program officer, Academy for Educational Development**

Invaluable for teachers across the curricula, this book shows you how to generate student initiative and excitement in the learning process and help students discover the purpose, power, and practice of writing.

This book offers teachers a Social Action instructional model for generating "real world" problem-solving and writing practice in or out of the classroom. The method can be applied to brief activities, long-term projects, or even "teachable moments," and encourages students to analyze problems collaboratively, develop action plans, discover solutions, and reflect on their work. The teacher, in turn, is encouraged to refrain from direct instruction, and instead let the students take initiative. Featuring stories by teachers who have successfully used the Social Action model, the book profiles various ways to apply the method across grade levels and content areas. Whether it's first graders mounting a letter writing campaign to improve their playground conditions or middle school students battling to save their school from demolition, the book shows how Social Action strategies can inspire student initiative in learning and help them acquire voice, authority, and passion for the writing process. The book's final section includes extensive project and activity ideas that teachers can undertake in the classroom.

The **NATIONAL WRITING PROJECT** (NWP) is a nationwide professional development program for teachers. Founded in 1974, its primary goal is to improve the teaching and learning of writing in the nation's schools. The NWP supports professional development activities, including over 12,000 teacher training consultants, operating through its writing project sites across the country. These sites collectively offer over 6,800 training programs to local schools and districts and serve about 130,000 teachers annually.

Other Books of Interest

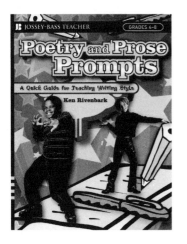

Poetry and Prose Prompts

A Quick Guide for Teaching Writing Style

Ken Rivenbark

Paper	ISBN: 978-0-7879-7879-2
	www.josseybass.com

"This book is an excellent resource for teachers striving to improve their students' writing as well as for college instructors who teach writing strategies. Rivenbark's own experiences as a teacher and teacher educator ensure that his approach is practitioner-oriented and developmental in nature."

—Carol Chase Thomas, associate dean, Watson School of Education, University of North Carolina at Wilmington

"Future writers of poetry and prose must be led to the proposition that more than intellect is involved. Ken Rivenbark has authored a convincing and persuasive insight into the challenge to the heart and soul which is central to great writing."

—Mary Jane Caylor, Alabama State Board of Education

A collection of outstanding and effective lessons, this book is the perfect resource to help teachers turn average writers into stellar authors. Learn how to address standards while fostering individual style and helping students to find their voices as authors. The book also includes valuable testing prompts, with examples from original or student-generated fiction.

Presented in an easy-to-use format, *Poetry and Prose Prompts* outlines for students all the skills needed to excel in writing practice. The book includes

- **Introduction to Poetry:** Haiku, Diamonte, Quatrains, Limericks, and Ballads
- **Introduction to Characterization:** Dialogues, Character Sketches, Biographical Sketches
- **Introduction to Narrative Writing:** Tall Tales, Short Stories, Fables, Fairy Tales, Spooky Stories, Autobiographical Incidents

Ken Rivenbark, listed in *Who's Who Among America's Top Teachers* (1998 & 2005), is the Director of Curriculum Development for Virtual Sage and former lecturer in the Watson School of Education at the University of North Carolina at Wilmington.

Other Books of Interest

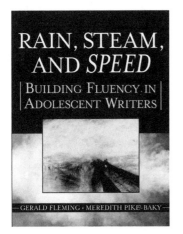

Rain, Steam, and Speed

Building Fluency in Adolescent Writers

Gerald Fleming & Meredith Pike-Baky

Paper	ISBN: 978-0-7879-7456-5
	www.josseybass.com

"With enormous pleasure and pride, the students in *Rain, Steam, and Speed* are writing more, faster, and better than they have ever written before. How to make, or let, that happen with our own students in our own classrooms is what Gerald Fleming and Meredith Pike-Baky have to teach us."

—William Slaughter, professor and chair, Department of English, University of North Florida, Jacksonville

Many books focus on teaching the technical skills and processes of writing, but few works address issues of *fluency*—how to help students write with ease and facility on a variety of topics. *Rain, Steam, and Speed* offers a carefully structured approach for helping students to overcome writing blocks so they can communicate quickly, confidently, and thoughtfully when the demand arises. Featuring over 150 writing prompts on provocative topics, the book includes everything a teacher needs to know to inspire and engage students in systematic writing practice, including classroom protocols, grading, assessment, and feedback approaches. Easily implemented in any English/language arts classroom, the program involves about one hour of instruction per week (ideally in half-hour segments), taking students through a series of timed writing exercises and enabling them to dramatically improve their thinking and writing facility over time. This guide:

- Offers structured process for improving student writing.
- Features over 150 provocative writing exercises.
- Includes extensive examples of student work (along with testimonials).
- Benefits all types of students, including English learners.
- Strengthens literacy skills for cross-content academic learning.
- Adapts to all levels of English/language arts classrooms.

Gerald Fleming is an award-winning teacher who has taught in the San Francisco Public Schools for over thirty years. He teaches English, social studies, and journalism, and also teaches curriculum and instruction at the University of San Francisco.

Meredith Pike-Baky is a curriculum and assessment coordinator, a teacher educator, and a teacher consultant with the Bay Area Writing Project.

Other Books of Interest

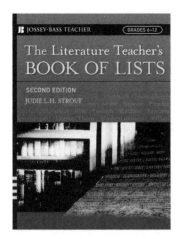

The Literature Teacher's Book of Lists

Second Edition

Judie L. H. Strouf

Paper   ISBN: 978-0-7879-7550-0
www.josseybass.com

"Judie Strouf's encyclopedic *Literature Teacher's Book of Lists* is truly amazing! I recommend it enthusiastically to all my students—especially those who are prospective teachers."
—Michael Flachmann, professor of English, California State University, Bakersfield and 1995 Carnegie Foundation United States Professor of the Year

"This quality resource of literature, especially for young adults, is beneficial for anyone—not strictly educators. Parents, and even students, might use Ms. Strouf's book in selecting appropriate reading materials. During this stage in education when reading at grade level is a serious problem, this reference would greatly assist anyone in need of such information."
—Cheri Zangmeister, English and reading teacher, Southern High School, Louisville, Kentucky

This comprehensive reference offers over 200 unique and time-saving lists for both teacher background and student use. With completely updated information, *The Literature Teacher's Book of Lists, Second Edition* offers brand-new and expanded sections, including:

- Lists addressing young adult concerns, such as divorce, eating disorders, and pregnancy
- Lists that highlight literature from a variety of ethnic groups, including African-American, Latino, and Asian
- Lists of the best literature from around the world
- Expanded reference lists offering teacher suggestions, research ideas, and the use of the Internet

These 254 lists are useful for developing instructional materials and planning lessons across grade levels. Some of the lists supply teacher background, others are reproducibles for student use, and many give new twists to studied topics. The sections include: literature • books • genres • poetry • drama • themes • literary periods • student activities • and teacher tips.

Judie Strouf spent 27 years as a teacher of language arts, literature, creative writing, and drama. She is the author of numerous successful books, including *Hooked on Language Arts!* (Jossey-Bass, 1990) and the first edition of *The Literature Teacher's Book of Lists* (Jossey-Bass, 1993). Now retired, she lives in Sun City West, Arizona.

Other Books of Interest

Teaching with Fire

Poetry that Sustains the Courage to Teach

Sam M. Intrator and Megan Scribner

Cloth	ISBN: 978-0-7879-6970-7
	www.josseybass.com

"Teaching with Fire is a glorious collection of the poetry that has restored the faith of teachers in the highest, most transcendent values of their work with children . . . Those who want us to believe that teaching is a technocratic and robotic skill devoid of art or joy or beauty need to read this powerful collection. So, for that matter, do we all."

—Jonathan Kozol, author of *Amazing Grace and Savage Inequalities*

Those of us who care about the young and their education must find ways to remember what teaching and learning are really about. We must find ways to keep our hearts alive as we serve our students. Poetry has the power to keep us vital and focused on what really matters in life and in schooling.

Teaching with Fire is a wonderful collection of eighty-eight poems from well-loved poets such as Walt Whitman, Langston Hughes, Billy Collins, Emily Dickinson, and Pablo Neruda. Each of these evocative poems is accompanied by a brief story from a teacher explaining the significance of the poem in his or her life's work. This beautiful book also includes an essay that describes how poetry can be used to grow both personally and professionally.

Teaching with Fire was written in partnership with the Center for Teacher Formation and the Bill & Melinda Gates Foundation. Royalties will be used to fund scholarship opportunities for teachers to grow and learn.

Sam M. Intrator (Northampton, MA) is associate professor of education and child study at Smith College. A former high school teacher, administrator, and son of two public school teachers, he is the editor of *Stories of the Courage to Teach, Living the Questions, and Leading from Within.*

Megan Scribner (Takoma Park, MD) is a freelance writer and editor who has worked with numerous foundations and educational organizations.